MELISSA'S MARVE[LOUS]
MEATLESS MEA[LS]

EVERYDAY RECIPES THAT ARE
FREE OF GLUTEN, DAIRY, AND
REFINED SUGAR

BY MELISSA PICKELL, R. D.

Published by:
New You Nutrition
49 Leffler Hill Road
Flemington, New Jersey 08822

www.pickellnutrition.com

Cover photographs and design by Deborah Gichan Photography, www.farmstudio.net

Food photographs by Frederic S. Bernstein and Susan Speak

Author photograph by Frederic S. Bernstein

Food illustrations by Christopher S. Pickell

First Edition – September 2008
ISBN 978-0-615-24319-1

Printed on partially recycled paper.

Disclaimer: The information contained in this book is not intended as medical advice. The author, publisher, and/or distributors will not assume responsibility for any adverse consequences resulting from these recipes.

For Zelda with love
November 28, 1935 - January 29, 1991

Foreword

As a physician I have devoted my career to helping people understand how their life style impacts their health. This understanding becomes useful only to the extent that it can be used to make meaningful changes in how we live. I believe that all physicians would like to offer this kind of advice if they only knew what exactly would be effective changes and how to implement those changes. Seeing improvements in their patients would be reinforcing and they would be motivated to learn more about this mode of practice.

Similarly, we as individuals would all like to feel better and be healthier if we only knew what would make that happen. Making any single change, such as jumping in place and swinging our arms, as with an imagined jump rope, might help someone feel more invigorated during the day. This might be motivating to try other life style changes.

If life style changes allowed someone to avoid a pharmaceutical treatment, for example if morning exercise lowered the blood pressure, then this would also be motivating.

All this probably sounds simplistic and a bit idealistic, yet it is indeed possible. Unfortunately most physicians are poorly trained in guiding lifestyle changes such as nutrition, and have not had positive experiences with giving dietary advice. In fact, the advice given is often non-specific and overly simplistic such as "eat less fat" or "cut down on calories."

The expectation is that the next visit, <u>when</u> the diet has failed, medications will be started. This nutritional nihilism is reinforced by repeated failures of "the diet approach" over the years of practice. Even practice guidelines, the recommendations to doctors regarding treatment approaches, give lip service to "lifestyle changes" as a first step, but never give any specific advice as to how to guide the patient in this pursuit.

Individuals have had similar repeated failures of dietary trials and have little expectation of long-term success. Thus the TV ads and bookshelves are full of the latest flirtations with dietary offerings.

One reason that diets fail in the long run is that they are "diets" and have little to do with lifestyle changes. When I suggest a diet for someone that is based on his or her long-term health needs or genetic makeup then it is essential that the diet be viewed as a vital part of a healthy future. The diet must be translated into a lifestyle that includes this new way of eating. Any life style change that is not full of love, fun and great tastes will not last. Otherwise, why would anyone bother to make the changes?

When it comes to dietary changes it is crucial to have a nutritionist available who can translate the dietary advice into that living, enjoyable life. If a diet change is going to be successful and last a lifetime then it must taste great and incorporate many familiar foods and recipes so there is not a chronic sense of loss and mourning.

Melissa Pickell is such a nutritionist. Over the years I have entrusted some of my most difficult nutrition challenges to her and have always been more than pleased with her range of suggestions. She loves to take a client's favorite recipes and convert them into a form that preserves the flavor and texture while avoiding problem foods.

This book comes out of her own journey, as she needed to develop a gluten- and casein-free life style for her loved one. For him, the alternative would have been dangerous drugs or serious surgery so the need was imperative. But to make it stick, the food had to be real and had to be palatable. Any diet that leaves you feeling like you are on a diet is doomed to failure, even if the alternatives are gloomy.

Many people learn very healthy gluten- and casein-free recipes, but to do so within the boundaries of a vegetarian diet is no small challenge. Between these covers, Melissa has delivered a very readable and eminently useful guide to shopping, preparing and cooking gluten- and casein-free food that nourishes both body and soul. That it is vegetarian is important for some, and merely an exciting addition for others, but no one will feel deprived with these incredibly delicious vegetarian meals.

Eating should be a time for quiet revelry in the joy of nourishing our body. A meal should excite our palate and please our mind. The ideal meal will promote health and leave us eager for the next meal. Within the pages of Melissa's Marvelous Meatless Meals, readers will learn practical tips and try tasty recipes that will enable them to not only <u>follow</u> a vegetarian, gluten- and casein-free lifestyle, but also to rekindle their excitement in the joy of food.

By Stuart H Freedenfeld, MD

Dr. Freedenfeld received his Medical Degree, with honors, from the College of Medicine and Dentistry of New Jersey in 1975. In 1988, Dr. Freedenfeld began studying herbal medicine, nutritional therapies and homeopathy. Over the years, he has gained expertise in traditional herbalism, Chinese herbalism, homeopathy, nutritional medicine and IV therapies such as chelation, and has become recognized as one of the leading experts in the integration of multiple forms of healing, with specialties in the areas of chronic fatigue, chronic pain, allergy, autoimmune disease, colitis, heart and cardiovascular diseases, diabetes, detoxification, longevity and health maintenance. He is devoted to integrating the finest aspects of healing arts from around the world and throughout time and passionately pursues this knowledge to provide the safest and most effective approaches to health and healing for his patients.

Foreword

Inside the Book

Knife's Lessons

Muffins, Pancakes, & Waffles

Side Salads & Soups

Dressings & Sauces

Main Dish Salads & Soups

Main Dishes

Simple Vegetable Sides

Snacks

Desserts

Internet Sources

Acknowledgements

Introduction

Why Write This Book?

Years ago when I decided that one day I would write a cookbook, I had a very different vision of what that book would be. I am a registered dietitian with a passion for helping my clients find wonderful foods that work within their particular diet restrictions. Although I have provided excellent, healthy, and tasty vegetarian meals for my family for years, we never had to contend with food allergies, or any dietary restrictions for health reasons. Over the years of raising my children I have grown many of the vegetables I have cooked, baked many types of bread, and experimented with all sorts of whole grains and other foods not commonly found on the typical American table.

I am founder of a unique private practice in weight loss coaching, diet makeovers, and teen weight management. Using a hands-on and practical approach, I work with individuals and families in their homes where I can evaluate the food items in the pantry, availability of cooking equipment to prepare healthful meals, and the cooking techniques used. Some sessions are held in the client's grocery store to demonstrate label reading and healthful food purchasing. Best of all, my clients really enjoy our cooking sessions together, where we prepare a few items; it is a great way for me to introduce fruits, vegetables, whole grains, and low fat preparation.

In addition to weight loss coaching, I work with clients who have various food restrictions and intolerances which result in gluten-free, dairy-free, and sugar-free diets. These restrictions add many other dimensions and complications to a person's daily lifestyle and become acute when traveling and during family celebrations and holidays.

Introduction

Some of these restrictions hit my own household when my husband, who was living with a chronic intestinal disorder, became frustrated with the lack of results from pharmaceutical medication and no particular diet. After seeking help from a wonderful holistic medical doctor, Chris began to follow a very restricted diet of no gluten, no dairy, no refined sugar, and for the first six months, no corn in any form. And did I mention that we are vegetarian? I remember sitting in the doctor's office and thinking, "OK, this is my profession, I can understand what all of these restrictions require, and I know how to research what to do". And then I went to the grocery store. I admit that I stood there and cried. In the health food section of the store, every package I picked up contained one or more of the ingredients that Chris wasn't allowed.

A gluten-free diet is complicated enough, but being vegetarian added some extra challenges. For gluten-free vegetarians, meal planning can be additionally complicated since almost all of the commercially available alternative protein sources contain wheat gluten and/or soy sauce which have wheat. No more veggie crumbles, veggie burgers, hot dogs, or seitan. Even certain types of tempeh are made with grains that have gluten.

I realized that I would need to prepare almost everything from scratch (which I was mostly doing already anyway) and I would have to be vigilant in label reading. Having been a bread baker most of my life, I tried my hand at gluten-free bread, very unsuccessfully. I needed a book on gluten-free baking. I purchased two cookbooks which were helpful in teaching me some of the principles of gluten-free baking, but I found that the available books included a lot of dairy and meat, the baked goods contained lots of refined sugar, and there were no recipes for some of the gluten-free whole grains that we were already using, like millet and buckwheat.

I combed the library shelves looking for books that suited our new nutritional lifestyle and found books that were vegetarian but not gluten-free, gluten-free but not dairy-free, sugar-free but not gluten- or dairy-free. An internet search for cookbooks containing recipes with no gluten, dairy, or refined sugar turned up one listing; however, one review of the book was by a frustrated person who complained that most of the recipes use brown sugar. Brown sugar is considered a refined sugar and my recipes do not contain this ingredient. My recipes use mostly honey, gluten-free brown rice syrup, and pure maple syrup as sweeteners, and occasionally concentrated fruit sweetener, date puree, or blackstrap molasses. Getting the texture, consistency, and taste right in a food that has no gluten, dairy, or granulated sugar is complicated and it is not surprising that people without a lot of kitchen know-how or professional nutrition experience would be overwhelmed.

Over many months I began to develop my own recipes, making adjustments to old family favorites, and creating new ones. I have since met many people, friends and clients, who follow a vegetarian lifestyle and are also trying to avoid processed sugars. I have received calls from potential clients who are overwhelmed by having many restrictions (and it seems the sugar restriction creates the greatest disturbance since sugar is in absolutely everything!) and not knowing how to eat anymore. I hope that my recipes are in keeping with the philosophy which I describe below: of eating healthfully and well, enjoying food, and promoting wholesome and home-prepared food. My recipes are not time consuming since I too have a busy family schedule. I hope my recipes will reach an audience of those who are trying to live a healthier lifestyle by cooking more, eating less meat, less wheat, and less sugar. In my home, we aim to cook a meal that works for everyone, regardless of their food restrictions. I have tried to take the recipes that we have enjoyed as a vegetarian family and find ways to make them dairy, gluten, and sugar free. My mother's delicious couscous recipe tastes just as good with a quinoa-millet base, and I have created a dairy-free cucumber soup that my children loved despite the hidden ingredient of silken tofu. I hope that my recipes will take some of the fear out of gluten-free vegetarian meal planning and put back some of the joy of eating.

My Philosophy

There are three main components to my philosophy about good nutrition: relearning to self-regulate food intake, reducing consumption of processed foods and replacing them with wholesome foods, and improving the quality of our food intake through better buying and better preparation, all of which increase our satisfaction.

I do not impose my own personal eating plan on others; I strongly believe that eating plans should be individualized and this is how I treat my clients. Although it is important to know what appropriate portion sizes look like, counting things (carbohydrates, calories, points, etc.) gives the feeling of being on a diet and is not sustainable for long periods of time. Many of my clients have lost the ability to self-regulate their food intake. In other words, they have become so conditioned to listen to external hunger cues (particular meal times, diet parameters, "shoulds and should nots") that they no longer know how to recognize their own hunger or recognize when they are satisfied. I work with clients to re-learn to recognize and listen to their body's internal hunger cues and to stop eating when they are satisfied.

I have worked with many families who have a regular diet of fast foods and highly processed packaged foods. From a nutritional perspective, the less a food is tampered with, the more nutritional value remains. I have never liked the idea of being at the mercy of the big food businesses which control much of what is presented to us in the food aisles. In New Jersey, we have an abundance of fresh fruits and vegetables from May through November and I encourage my clients to buy locally whenever possible. Buying locally grown (or even from within the same state if not from around the corner) fruits and vegetables means less time on the road losing nutrients, less truck time expending gas and pollution, supporting small farmers instead of agribusiness, and the quality and taste are unbeatable. In many European cities, farmers' markets are held a few times a week; Europeans wouldn't think of buying their produce at an impersonal market when there was fresher, tastier fare available. And consider the satisfaction quotient of home prepared versus packaged and processed. One really good homemade chocolate chip cookie is far more satisfying than four processed, packaged, store-bought chocolate chip cookies. I believe that is why many of us cannot stop eating after we've had a reasonable portion; our food has become so unsatisfying with too much salt, too much sugar, and lots of chemicals.

Personally, I feel that good nutrition should be a priority for individuals and families; we are given one body to abuse or take great care of and feeding that body is something we do at least three times a day for a lifetime, potentially 87,600 feedings! So why are we more concerned with the time we reserve for watching TV than the time we spend preparing to feed our one and only body? Eating healthfully **absolutely** takes more time and planning than the grab-n-go culture but there are many ways to make it fit into our busy lives.

What You Will Find in This Book

In Melissa's Marvelous Meatless Meals, mostly you will find recipes that are easy enough for every day cooking, and tasty enough to satisfy. The recipes are vegetarian, gluten-free, dairy-free, and have no refined sugar. Not all the recipes are vegan, though some are. In many cases, I have provided suggestions for making the food vegan, and for eliminating eggs for egg-allergic people. Although I have provided some brief explanations about gluten and other ingredients, I have kept these to a minimum. I have made the recipes wholesome by using healthful fats in healthful amounts, and by using a variety of vegetables, legumes, and some sea vegetables and fermented foods like miso and tempeh. Some of these ingredients may be new to you. I encourage you to experiment with an open mind. Many of my recipes are derived from different countries and cultures; most cultures around the world supply a vast number of meatless meals that are fabulously interesting. Lastly, I have provided some basic lessons about gluten-free baking without dairy and sugar. I hope you will try some new foods and enjoy a satisfying healthful diet every day whether or not you have ingredient restrictions. Enjoy!

In the Future

I am already at work on future books and would love to include your favorite recipes. Please send a recipe for a possible makeover to me at: www.pickellnutrition.com .
Please include your name and location so I can credit your contribution.

Eliminating Gluten and Dairy

Following is a brief explanation about the terms gluten-free and casein-free and a primer on label reading.

What is gluten?

Gluten is the protein in the cereal grains wheat, rye and barley, and any food products containing these ingredients. Triticale, durum, semolina, kamut, & spelt are all forms of wheat so are not allowed.

What about oats?

Although oats have been used on gluten-free diets outside of the United States for years, they have not been recommended in the U.S. until recently because of the potential for contamination of the oats during harvesting and processing. There are now a few companies that certify their oats as gluten-free via the Gluten Free Certification Organization (GFCO). Check them out at these web sites: www.giftsofnature.net , www.creamhillestates.com, and www.bobsredmill.com . Some people with celiac disease do not tolerate oats, even if they are gluten-free.

How do I read labels for gluten?

Foods containing gluten can be labeled in many ways, some of them hidden. Sometimes wheat gluten is an ingredient in a food product and is listed as such. Avoid any foods that have any form of wheat, rye, oats, or barley listed. Make sure the label says "gluten-free."

Watch out for these hidden sources of gluten

Caramel color (may be made from barley)

Dextrin (may be made from wheat but **usually** made from corn)

Hydrolyzed vegetable protein, textured vegetable protein

Malt, malt flavoring (made from barley), malt vinegar

Modified food starch

      (unless the label specifies the source as corn)

Soy sauce (unless the label specifies "wheat-free")

When in doubt, call the company first
Food companies are used to getting calls and e-mails from concerned consumers. For this book, I called and spoke with several companies regarding their products. If ever you are dissatisfied with an answer and are unsure about a food, it is best not to eat it. When I spoke with Miso Master about their miso products, I asked them to explain the process by which the miso is made to determine if there were non-gluten-free grains used.

What is the difference between dairy, lactose, and casein?

Dairy refers to foods made from milk, cream, and milk products. Casein refers to the protein in milk and lactose is the sugar in milk. Dairy-free is not always casein-free. Many non-dairy foods contain casein in some form, for example some non-dairy cheeses contain calcium caseinate, a form of casein. Casein is found in cow, goat, and sheep milk, so all food products derived from these milks must be avoided.

What foods contain casein?
Milk
Cream
Puddings
Creamed soups
Half and half
Yogurt
Sour cream
Butter
Sherbet
Ice cream
Ice milk
Cheese
Anything with cheese

How do I read labels for casein?

Casein may be hidden in margarine, canned tuna, dairy-free cheese, and semi-sweet chocolate. Kosher pareve foods tend to be casein-free as they are free of dairy products.
For people with milk allergy, a trace of dairy protein can cause serious reactions. Some people will need to make sure any foods purchased are labeled that they were made in a facility that is dedicated as dairy-free. In other words, the equipment is guaranteed to have no trace of milk protein; the equipment is either cleaned between uses or the facility does not produce any products containing certain allergens.

In this book, I have not addressed the specific needs of food allergic people. If you have serious food allergies (resulting in anaphylaxis or other serious reactions), please make sure you read labels vigilantly, consult with a dietitian who specializes in food allergies, and join a food allergy support network. (www.foodallergy.org)

Resources for those who are new to the gluten free/casein free diet

There is a wealth of information available at the web sites of organizations like the Celiac Disease Foundation which I will not be addressing in detail in this book. I would urge you to seek information at these web sites to fully educate yourself about the many issues involved in living a gluten-free life.

A wealth of information can be found at:

www.csaceliacs.org
Celiac sprue association.

www.celiac.org
Celiac disease foundation.

www.triumphdining.com
A listing of gluten free restaurants and menus with special
dining cards to help explain restrictions to servers and chefs.

www.foodallergy.org
Food Allergy Network

www.gfcfdiet.com
For families with autism and those with celiac disease.

www.tacanow.com
TACA stands for "Talk About Curing Autism".
Families with autism helping families with autism.

Cross contamination issues in a gluten-free kitchen

There are many reasons for following a diet free of gluten
which include Celiac Disease, gluten intolerance that is not
celiac disease, and chronic intestinal disorders such as
inflammatory bowel disease and irritable bowel syndrome. The
degree of sensitivity to gluten is very individual and some
people are less bothered by a trace of gluten that may
accidentally have gotten into their food; in fact, they may not
even know a food has been cross-contaminated because there
is no reaction at all. However, for some people, including those
with celiac disease, a trace of gluten can mean days of work
lost, not to mention pain and discomfort.

Cross contamination is the term used to describe when any
amount of the ingredient or food which is being strictly
avoided finds its way into food somewhat "accidentally". For
example, a restaurant that grilled bread for a panini and then
grilled the allergic person's fish may "contaminate" the fish
with unwanted crumbs of gluten. Or perhaps the restaurant
cooked the chicken without any flour but cooked it in a skillet
that had flour in it and still had a trace left. A friend, who has
two immediate family members with Celiac, told me a story

about her friend who carefully prepared a "gluten-free" meal but used a wooden spoon; wood is very porous and apparently it had traces of flour from previous baking. This caused days of distress to my friend's daughter.

So here are a few things to think about when preparing gluten free food in your kitchen, especially if not everyone in the household is gluten-free and therefore you have ingredients with gluten *as well as* without.

- Keep gluten-free flour mixes in their own containers, not previously used.
- If someone in your house is very gluten sensitive, consider getting rid of all your wooden spoons and wooden cutting boards.
- Cook gluten-free pancakes first, before cooking non-gluten-free pancakes. Or designate certain cooking equipment, like pans, as gluten-free.
- Get cookie sheets that can be washed thoroughly to avoid contamination by non-gluten-free baking.
- Consider using paper muffin liners to avoid contamination.
- If the members of the household are all using the same bread spreads like peanut butter, soy margarine, almond butter, jam etc. make sure the rule is to take some out and not double dip after spreading on the bread which is how unwanted crumbs can get into the tub of peanut butter or margarine. Or have two of everything and label one as exclusively for the gluten-free person.
- A piece of wheat toast casually set down on a cutting board and then taken away can leave a few suspicious crumbs that may cause problems.
- Make sure that only clean plates and dishes are used for gluten-free foods. It may not be enough to wipe off wheat bread crumbs to re-use a plate.
- Label everything carefully. Two sets of leftover pancakes that are unlabeled can be a problem waiting to happen.

- ***Never*** use a sifter that has had regular flour in it. You will need a new sifter for gluten-free baking. Keep the gluten-free sifter in a plastic bag, labeled and tightly closed.

There are many more things to think about that I have not listed. If you are new to a gluten-free way of life, I would encourage you to visit one of the web sites that I mentioned to learn more about cross contamination.

Good Nutrition Tips for Healthy Vegetarians

Eating Well as a Vegetarian

We have all known people who are vegetarian and eat potato chips and brownies for lunch because these foods have no meat. You are probably not one of those people since you are reading this book.

I have read the blogs of vegetarians who eat a lot of starchy foods, very little protein, and don't vary their vegetable intake very much. Being vegetarian does not mean the best food choices are automatic. It takes effort to find balance, include protein foods, and vary our diet.

At the end of this section I have listed some daily menu ideas. Also in this section you will find *Building a Healthy Salad*. Eating a large "salad with everything", i.e. protein, carbohydrate, healthy fats, and lots of flavor, is one of the best ways I know of to improve your intake of vitamins and minerals, omega-3s and antioxidants. I have one of these "everything" salads almost every day and encourage you to do this as often as you can. I have given a few tips on reducing preparation time.

Vegetarians, particularly those also restricted by gluten and dairy, have very little room in their daily intake for empty calories. Make every meal and snack count as something good that you are giving your body.

Be mindful of fat and sugar intake. Emphasize fresh fruits and vegetables and try to include some of the vegetarian super foods that I discuss further in this section. Whenever possible choose whole foods over processed. Those foods you make at home will have less sodium, less fat, healthier fat, more fiber, and better nutrition, not to mention that they taste better too.

Why Should We Reduce or Eliminate Our Consumption of Refined Sugars?

There are plenty of reasons to reduce our intake of sugar. Refined sugars eaten in large amounts contribute to the acidity of the body which may lead to inflammation and immune system depression. Sugar provides no nutrients other than calories. And sugar can cause a quick rise in blood sugar followed by a low, which some people find affects their concentration and gives them physical symptoms of shakiness, sleepiness, or irritability.

In my work with individuals trying to lose weight, I have found that the need for sugar and sweet foods seems to build on itself. When we eat sugary foods, we often want more and more, but if we can satisfy our sweet craving with more natural forms of sugar like dried fruits which have less impact on our blood sugar, it is easier to control ourselves. Many of my clients find that after a few weeks of avoiding foods with refined sugars, their cravings are reduced and they are more easily satisfied with dried fruit snacks and fruit shakes.

We all enjoy having treats. In this book you will find recipes for cookies and desserts that use gluten-free brown rice syrup, pure maple syrup, agave nectar, honey, and date puree. Though these sweeteners are all forms of sugar and will have *some* impact on the blood sugar, there may be less of an extreme. By making and tasting some of these treats with alternative sweeteners, I hope you will feel better about what you are eating.

All About Fats

Blood fats
Blood fats, the ones circulating in your body, include total cholesterol, LDL cholesterol, HDL cholesterol, and triglycerides. You may or may not have had your cholesterol levels checked. Here is what these terms mean:

Total cholesterol
Too much cholesterol in the blood can clog arteries

LDL (bad) cholesterol
Low density lipoprotein, a mix of cholesterol and protein moving through the bloodstream, is main source of arterial plaque buildup (clogged arteries!)

HDL (good) cholesterol
High density lipoprotein carries cholesterol away from arteries and back to the liver so it can be eliminated from the body

Triglycerides
Associated with high cholesterol and heart disease though they don't contribute to plaque buildup.

Trans Fats
Trans fats increase your risk of heart disease more than any other source of calories
Trans fats are in your diet in the form of:
>   Fast foods
>   Packaged snack foods
>   Cookies, crackers, and other baked goods made with
>   hydrogenated (hardened) vegetable oils
Trans fats increase harmful LDL cholesterol
Trans fats decrease beneficial HDL cholesterol
Trans fats promote inflammation
Although food manufacturers are required to list the trans fats on labels, if a food contains less than 500 mgs of trans fat per serving, it can be labeled as zero. Therefore, several servings of hidden trans fats per day can add up to a negative impact on your heart.

To eliminate trans fats, avoid processed foods, especially foods that contain partially hydrogenated fats/oils.

Omega-3s
Omega-3s lower triglycerides, reduce blood pressure and boost arterial function
Eicosapentaenoic acid (EPA) & Docosahexaenoic acid (DHA) are the 2 omega-3 fatty acids found in fish oil
>Two 4-oz servings of fatty fish (salmon, mackerel, sardines) per week is recommended for those who eat fish

Alpha-linolenic acid (ALA) is the non-flesh source of omega-3s
>ALA is found in walnuts, flaxseeds and canola oil
>The body converts only 10-15 % of ALA into omega-3s

Vegetarian Superfoods

Beans, lentils (legumes)
Beans and lentils are an excellent low fat source of protein and fiber, which will help keep you feeling full long after you've finished your meal. Lentils are easy to store dry and are also quick cooking. Dried beans usually need to be soaked overnight in water to cover and then cooked before using in a recipe. Add a 2-3 inch piece of kombu sea vegetable to the soaking and cooking water to help soften the beans and aid in digestion.

Flax seed
Good source of Omega-3 fatty acids when ground flax is used. Flax seed may be purchased whole or ground; I prefer to buy it whole and grind small amounts which I keep in a jar in the refrigerator. Use ground flax on salads, cereal, and in pancakes, waffles and muffins. Whole flax seed has the benefit of fiber but is not broken down by the intestines. 3 Tablespoons of flax seed contains about 4 grams Omega-3's. Refrigerate flax seed after opening. Store freshly ground flax seed in the refrigerator.

Hemp seed
2 Tablespoons raw, shelled hemp seed provides all 9 essential amino acids, 6 grams protein, 1 gram fiber, and 2 grams

Omega-3 ALA. Hemp is not grown in the U.S. but is imported from Canada where it is grown on the prairies. Most of the hemp grown in Canada is organic. Hemp is also available in the form of protein powder, nut butter, flour, and hemp milk, a non-dairy milk. The seeds taste a lot like sunflower seeds and can be sprinkled on cereal, salads, and vegetables. Hemp seed products can be purchased via www.nutiva.com, www.livingharvest.com and www.rawganique.com.

Miso

Miso is a fermented soy food, a staple in Japanese cooking. Its health benefits include alkalizing the blood (reducing inflammation) and providing isoflavones, a powerful phytochemical (from plants). Miso also contains lactobacillus bacteria and enzymes which aid digestion. Miso has been shown to have 20 times as much isoflavones per gram of soy protein as unfermented soy foods like soymilk and tofu. Miso can be made into a simple, brothy soup with vegetables, tofu, and seaweed (see recipes) or added to dressings, sauces, and spreads.

According to Great Eastern Sun, the makers of Miso Master Organic Miso, the following flavors of miso are gluten-free:

> Organic Chickpea Miso (soy-free)
> Organic Sweet White Miso
> Organic Brown Rice Miso
> Organic Mellow White Miso
> Organic Traditional Red Miso

In my recipes, I have used Organic Mellow White Miso which I find to be very mild tasting. Miso is made by inoculating a grain with aspergillus spore (koji) and then mixing this with cooked soybeans and allowing it to "age" and ferment. Some koji is made with barley (not gluten-free), some with rice. Be sure to find out what grain is used to make the koji if you are partial to a particular brand of miso. www.great-eastern-sun.com

Nutritional yeast
Nutritional yeast is inactive yeast which is yellow and has a somewhat cheesy taste. There are some great recipes for vegan cheese which use raw nuts and nutritional yeast as ingredients. It is also good on salad, sprinkled on pasta, or popcorn. Nutritional yeast boasts 8 grams of protein per $1\frac{1}{2}$ Tbsp, and is enhanced with B-vitamins, including B-12 which is absent from vegan diets.
Red Star Nutritional Yeast is gluten-free according to LeSaffre Yeast Corporation.

Sea Vegetables
Sea vegetables are part of a large family of marine algae. Seaweeds have long been used in Asian medicine as healing foods. They provide a pretty good source of iodine and vitamin K, folate, and magnesium, and smaller amounts of iron, calcium, riboflavin and pantothenic acid. But not much is needed; Asian cultures use seaweeds as a condiment rather than a side dish. Only 2 Tbsp or so is needed to provide the healthy benefits.

My Favorite Ways to Use Sea Vegetables:

Kombu
Place a 2 to 3-inch piece of kombu in with dried beans while soaking overnight and then add it to the pot while the beans are cooking, to tenderize the beans and aid in digestion.
Use a 2 to 3-inch piece of Kombu for making dashi, the broth used to make miso soup

Dulse
Pan-fry in a little olive oil and eat on sandwich with pan-fried tofu , tomato, and vegan mayo.
Dulse can also be dry-fried in a skillet over a medium-low flame; cook until the red dulse turns light brown; makes a salty, crunchy snack.

Wakame
Add 1-2 tsp instant wakame to miso soup.

Arame
Mild-tasting black strings; soak and then add to stir-fries and salads.

Nori
Roasted nori is used to make sushi. If you haven't tried making this at home, it is really easy and very delicious. You will use sushi rice seasoned with rice vinegar and brown rice syrup and wrap this along with raw julienne vegetables.
Another delicious and simple way to enjoy nori seaweed is to snip it using a kitchen scissors over a bowl of brown rice.

Soy foods
Soy foods are the main dietary source of isoflavones, natural chemicals thought to have disease-fighting effects. High quality sources of soy isoflavones include tofu, tempeh, edamame, and soy milk. Many soy-based meat substitutes contain textured soy protein which is not the best source. Additionally, many of these convenience foods, (soy meats like sausage, bologna, pepperoni etc.) also contain wheat gluten.

Tempeh
Not only is Tempeh a vegetarian superfood providing soy isoflavones, protein and fiber, it is also in the category of "fermented foods." Fermented foods such as tempeh, miso, saurkraut and kimchee as well as cultured foods like yogurt contain beneficial microorganisms called probiotics. Probiotics, or "good bacteria", supply enzymes that aid in digestion, boost immunity, and may help to reduce sensitivity responses to food. You will find more detailed nutritional information and a delicious way to enjoy tempeh in the Main Dish recipe for *Tempeh Bacon BLT.*

Buying Organic and Local

There are many reasons to buy organic, including health and the environment. Every time we buy organic foods, we are sending a message to big food manufacturers and agribusinesses that we want better farming practices which impact our environment less and produce chemical-free foods for our bodies. In my introduction I said that we are given only one body to take care of or abuse with our food intake, exercise habits, and lifestyle choices. We have been given only one Earth to take care of too. We all need to work together to do more to influence how our food is produced, marketed, shipped, and purchased, to minimize the impact on this one and only Earth.

Local food is not necessarily organic. For me, local food mostly refers to local produce in my area which is available from May through November. Check your area for Farmer's Markets, farm stands, and locally grown produce sold in the grocery store. The fewer miles your fruits and vegetables have to travel, the fresher and better tasting it will be and the more nutritional value will be retained; not to mention fewer exhaust fumes were emitted to get your food to market. At our local Farmer's Market, the farmers will often tell me that a particular vegetable was picked that morning. Buying locally will also open your palate to varieties of fruits and vegetables that are not commonly sold in large supermarkets such as heirloom tomatoes and white peaches.

Raw Food Diets

My profession as a nutrition counselor has taken me in some interesting directions. Lately, I've been experimenting with the Raw Food Diet in hopes of finding some food options for my clients with many ingredient restrictions. Raw foodists, as those who follow a raw food diet are called, eat anywhere from 60-100% raw food on a daily basis. The approaches to this way of eating are as diverse as there are diets to follow, and there are many reasons for eating raw foods including weight loss, food allergies, and a desire to increase energy. The premise is that our foods contain the most nutrients and enzymes *before* they're cooked; therefore nothing on the raw food diet is heated above 118 degrees. Foods are either raw, dried without preservatives, sprouted, soaked, or dehydrated.

Personally, though I eat a lot of raw foods (fresh fruits, vegetables, nuts, and seeds), I don't subscribe to a 100% raw food plan. It is hard to get excited about cold soup during the winter in the northeast, and there are plenty of healthy *hot* options to choose from. But along the path of searching for alternatives for my severely restricted clients, I've discovered quite a few wonderful, delicious recipes; no flour, no dairy, no eggs—only fruits, nuts, spices, and sweetened with dates so the desserts are actually *healthy*. You will find recipes for raw treats in both the Snacks and Desserts sections.

Building a Healthy Salad

Having a colorful raw vegetable salad every day is a great way to get vitamins and minerals and a boost of antioxidants, lean protein, fiber, and healthy fats.

Choose any combination of the following:

<u>Greens</u>
radicchio
baby spinach
mesclun greens
lettuce, dark leafy
Belgian endive

Good Nutrition Tips for Healthy Vegetarians

Shredded vegetables
Shredded, chopped, or sliced carrots (slice baby carrots as a time saver, or buy pre-shredded carrots)
shredded raw beets
shredded red cabbage or coleslaw mix
broccoli slaw (prepackaged)

Add some of these other vegetables
scallions
red onion
radishes
sundried tomatoes (dried, not packed in oil),
        soak in boiling water first
tomatoes
grape tomatoes, cherry tomatoes
cucumber
peppers, all colors
leftover broccoli or cooked/grilled vegetables
leftover cooked potatoes or sweet potatoes
sprouts — alfalfa, broccoli sprouts— **Beware** of gluten in sprouted grains!
celery
Jerusalem artichoke, sliced

Add one or two of the following proteins
tofu (1/5 container Extra Firm)
homemade baked tofu
homemade tempeh bacon or tempeh fajita strips
1 hard boiled egg
chickpeas ($\frac{1}{4}$ - $\frac{1}{2}$ cup)
kidney beans ($\frac{1}{4}$ - $\frac{1}{2}$ cup)
black beans ($\frac{1}{4}$ - $\frac{1}{2}$ cup)
1-4 Tbsp hummus
cooked lentils
lentil spread

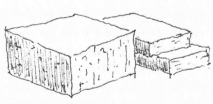

Add one of the following "good" fats
1 Tbsp sunflower seeds (raw)
1 Tbsp tahini (sesame paste)
1 Tbsp your favorite nuts (cashews, pecans, walnuts)
1 tsp olive oil (mix with 2 tsp lemon juice or flavored vinegar)
a few olives
avocado or guacamole

Optional Fruit Additions
dried unsweetened blueberries
fresh blueberries
sliced strawberries
fresh pear, sliced
raisins, dried fruit-sweetened cranberries, and blueberries
fresh apple, sliced
peeled and sliced citrus fruit (Clementine, orange, grapefruit)
grapes, whole or halved
lemon zest

Fresh Herbs
Parsley, fresh basil or any other of your favorite fresh herbs

Time saving tips
Make a salad mix for the week consisting of:
lettuce, spinach, and/or mesclun *(try some pre-packaged greens mixes)*
shredded cabbage *(available shredded or buy the coleslaw mix package)*
grated carrot *(available pre-shredded)*, broccoli slaw *(available packaged)*, chopped herbs like parsley or fresh basil when they are in season.

Only use "dry" vegetables in this salad base. Add "wet" vegetables like cucumber and tomatoes as you make your salad each day.

Try to pre-cut some veggies like baby carrots, peppers, celery, etc. and keep these in separate bags or containers.

Daily Menu Ideas

Here are just a few ideas for menus to show how to balance a meal with protein, carbohydrate, and fat, and incorporate some of the superfoods and recipes mentioned in this book. The portion sizes will vary depending on age and activity level.

Breakfast Ideas

- 1 serving gluten-free hot cereal or gluten-free oatmeal, topped with 2 teaspoons of ground flax seed or hemp seed, chopped apple, banana, peach, or berries, 1 teaspoon raw sunflower seeds, pumpkin seeds, or sliced almonds, and soy milk. Rice cakes with hummus, sliced cucumber and alfalfa sprouts.

- 2 gluten-free frozen waffles with fruit sweetened apple butter. 1 container flavored soy yogurt mixed with 1 cup mixed fruits and 1-2 teaspoons ground flax, 1 teaspoon sliced almonds or sunflower seeds.

- Gluten-free muffin (homemade) with a fruit and soymilk shake.

- Gluten-free cereal bar (see Snacks for Peanut Butter Cereal Bar recipe), soy yogurt with chopped fresh fruits, and 1-2 teaspoons ground flax.

- Tofu scramble with vegetables (see Main Dishes for Tofu Scramble recipe), Kinnikinnick gluten-free casein-free sesame bagel, toasted, with almond butter.

- Tempeh Bacon BLT (Main Dishes); fresh fruit.

- Vegetable omelet, and gluten-free muffin or gluten-free toast with fruit-sweetened jam.

- Gluten-free pancakes with fruit topping or pure maple syrup. Serve with tempeh bacon or egg for extra protein if desired.

- Homemade gluten-free waffles with fruit topping. Serve with Tofu Ricotta Crème for extra protein.

- Gluten-free cereal with soymilk, and topped with berries, peach, or banana. Serve with a slice of gluten-free toast spread with almond butter and fruit sweetened jam.

Lunch Ideas
- Large "Everything Salad"- ¼ cup hummus, 2 ounces smoked tofu, mesclun greens, leftover new potato, shredded carrot, a few grape tomatoes, a few slices of cucumber and green pepper, 1-2 Tbsp snipped Nori seaweed, 1-2 tsp olive oil, lemon juice or vinegar.

- Sandwich of gluten-free bread, hummus, thin slices of tomato, cucumber, and roasted red pepper; serve with fresh fruit.

- Tempeh Bacon BLT (Main Dishes); fresh fruit.

- Leftover bean or lentil soup, side salad with just raw veggies, fresh fruit, rice cake with hummus or peanut butter.

- Leftover pureed soup, rice crackers with lentil spread, small side salad with 2 oz tofu cubes, fresh fruit.

- Basic Miso Soup (Side Salads and Soups), leftover brown rice with tofu and vegetables.

- 1 slice of gluten-free toast with sliced hard boiled egg and sliced cucumber, some raw veggies with bean dip, chopped fruit topped with soy yogurt and sunflower seeds.

Snacks
See extensive snack idea list in the Snacks section

Dinner Ideas
There are many tasty and easy dinner recipes in the Main Dish and Main Dish Soups and Salads sections. I have also tried to provide serving suggestions along with the recipes. I often cook the dinner meal with an eye toward leftovers which we enjoy the next day for lunch. When there are lots of containers of leftovers in the refrigerator we will plan a "leftover night", usually reserved for the busiest night of the week when everyone goes in different directions.

What is in My Gluten-Free Kitchen?

Listed below are many of the ingredients that I keep on hand in my kitchen and that I have used in this book. If you are new to gluten-free cooking or baking with unrefined sugars, I do not recommend that you go out and stock your kitchen with every ingredient that I have listed here. Rather, purchase items on an as-needed basis to begin with.

Ingredients

Soy Foods
Tempeh
> Lite Life or other brand; check to make sure it is gluten-free. Extras can be kept frozen

Silken tofu, vacuum-packed
> (use for dressings, smoothies, and adding creaminess to recipes)

Extra firm lite or extra firm tofu
Plain soymilk (for baking)
Vanilla soymilk (for cereal and smoothies)
Soy yogurt, various flavors
Tofu Pups by Lite Life Foods
> gluten-free per the company

Wild Wood Tofu-Veggie Burgers

Frozen Veggie Burgers
Sunshine Burger (sunflower seeds, brown rice, carrots, herbs)
Sunrich Naturals Classic Soy Veggie Burger and Portabello Mushroom Veggie Burger

What is in My Gluten-Free Kitchen?

Frozen Gluten-free Waffles & Breads
Van's wheat-free, gluten-free waffles
      (original and apple with cinnamon)
Lifestream buckwheat, gluten-free waffles
      (blueberries and raspberries)
Kinnikinnick Sunflower Flax Rice Bread, Italian White Tapioca
Rice Bread, Tapioca Rice Hamburger Buns
Garbo Sun Bread or Garbo Bio Bread
Glutino Gluten-free Flax Seed Bread or Glutino Gluten-free
Fiber Bread

Seasonings
Nutritional yeast; Red Star brand is gluten-free per the
company
Dijon mustard
Vegan mayonnaise
Miso; (Eastern Sun is gluten-free per the company)
Mirin (rice cooking wine)
Wasabi powder
San-J wheat-free soy sauce
Rice vinegar
Red wine vinegar
Raspberry vinegar
White wine vinegar
Apple cider vinegar
Balsamic vinegar

Oils & Fats
Ghee by Purity Farms is gluten-, lactose- and casein-free
      (adds a buttery flavor to baking) but not vegan
Canola oil, store brand, for baking
Misto pump spray filled with extra virgin olive oil
Extra virgin olive oil, LARGE size
Toasted sesame oil

Dried Beans
Brown lentils
Red lentils
Dried black beans

Pasta & Noodles
100% buckwheat soba noodles
Wide rice noodles (Thai)
Thin rice noodles (rice sticks)
Gluten-free pasta: we like Tinkayada Brown Rice Pasta
Rice flour Vietnamese spring roll wrappers
> (if you are very sensitive to gluten, check with the company before using as they may have cross-contamination from other flours)

Rice & Gluten-Free Grains
Amaranth, whole grain
Short grain brown rice
Brown basmati rice
White basmati rice
Jasmine rice
Sushi rice, white or brown
Organic white rice
Wild rice
Quinoa, whole grain
Buckwheat groats, whole
Millet, whole
Teff, whole grain

Sea Vegetables
Nori
> 8-inch sheets, toasted, for sushi
> Also can be used for replacing anchovies or fish in recipes or snipped into fine pieces as a topping for grains

What is in My Gluten-Free Kitchen?

Arame

>   Mild flavored sea vegetable, great for stir-fries and
>   salads

Kombu

>   2-3 inch piece added to dried beans during soaking and
>   cooking helps to tenderize the beans and aids in
>   digestion

Dulse

>   Dry toast and add to green salads
>   "Fry" in olive oil until brown for a crispy seaweed chip

Wakame

>   Instant, for miso soup and stir-fries

Agar flakes

>   To replace animal gelatin

Unrefined Sweeteners

Blackstrap Molasses

Gluten-free brown rice syrup

>   (Lundberg makes gluten-free brown rice syrup)

Wax Orchards concentrated fruit juice

>   (Can be used as a sweetener for fruit-type desserts in
>   place of honey, maple syrup, or gluten-free brown rice
>   syrup).

Pure maple syrup

Local honey

>   Health benefits from local honey include providing
>   some immunity from environmental allergies like
>   grasses, trees and pollen which are local to a
>   geographical area

Date sugar

>   A dry sugar made from pulverized dried dates, great
>   for streusel toppings and fruit crisps

Maple sugar

>   A dry sugar, great for streusel toppings and fruit
>   crisps

Agave nectar

>   Honey-like consistency but milder flavor and vegan,
>   comes from the agave cactus plant

Nuts & Seeds
Ground flax seed
>Sprinkle on hot rice cereal and salads, or add to muffins, pancakes, and waffles for a healthy dose of vegetarian Omega-3 fatty acids

Raw sesame seeds
Raw sunflower seeds
Almonds, whole, sliced, slivered
Pecans
Walnuts
Tahini (sesame paste or butter)
Almond butter, raw or toasted
Peanut butter, natural, unsweetened, store brand
Hemp Seed

Dried Fruits
Pitted dates
>For making date puree or for making fruit-nut snacks

Dark raisins
A variety of other dried fruits, not necessarily all at the same time, including:
>Juice-sweetened cranberries
>Juice-sweetened blueberries
>Dried cherries
>Currants
>Dried apricots
>Mission figs (my favorite!)

Canned Vegetables
Chickpeas
Black beans
Dark red kidney beans
Fat free, vegetarian, refried beans
Pinto beans
Diced tomatoes, medium and large size cans
Tomato paste
White beans

What is in My Gluten-Free Kitchen?

<u>Gluten-Free Flours & Baking Ingredients</u>
Sorghum flour, superfine (Authentic Foods)
Corn flour
Buckwheat flour
Superfine brown rice flour (Authentic Foods)
Garbanzo flour
Millet flour
Tapioca starch flour
Potato starch flour
Almond flour (Almond meal)
Aluminum-free baking powder
Xanthan gum
Vanilla extract
Espresso powder

<u>Dairy-Free Chocolate</u>
Unsweetened cocoa powder
Gluten-free, dairy-free chocolate chips such as Enjoy Life or
Tropical Source

Tools You Can Use

I like to keep things fairly simple, and, personally, it bothers me when recipes call for some kind of special equipment that is only used for one particular food. For example, I have a cookbook that calls for a stove-top smoker, and another raw food cookbook calls for a food dehydrator. I have tried to list the kitchen equipment that I would say I could not do without or that really make food preparation easier. Chances are you may already have many of these items.

Blender
A basic blender is needed for shakes, pureeing soups, and making dressings.

Box grater
The box grater is 'great' for quick grating jobs that don't require taking out the food processor and then washing it.

Chopsticks
Although they are not used for cooking, I include them because they are fun to use for eating Asian style meals. They are also a great weight control tool! Chopsticks slow down your eating and force you to take smaller bites.

Egg slicer
Like a guillotine, this little device uses a series of wires to cut hard-boiled eggs into perfect slices. Slices bananas too.

Food processor
I couldn't do what I do in the kitchen without my food processor. It allows me to grate large quantities of carrots for salad, chop nuts, blend tofu, puree date paste, make hummus, and many other tasks. It makes all of this fast and easy and not a terrible chore.

Tools You Can Use

Good cutting boards
Wood is non-slippery and therefore great for cutting vegetables and chopping nuts and garlic safely. Caution should be taken to avoid cross contamination with wooden cutting boards, see **Cross Contamination Issues in a Gluten-Free Kitchen.**
It is also convenient to have a thick plastic cutting board that can be put in the dishwasher.

Knives and knife sharpener
If you don't already have them, get a good set of knives. You need at least one paring knife, a serrated edge knife, a slicing knife, and possibly a chef's knife for chopping nuts or garlic. See **Knife's Lessons** for knife techniques.
I find my Chef's Choice knife sharpener invaluable and very easy to use. There are two types, one for serrated, and I have the one for non-serrated knives. To use the sharpener, run the knife back and forth in each slot 10-15 times. Using properly sharpened knives will allow you to slice tomatoes into very thin slices, as well as a host of other knife tasks.

Lemon juicer
I have a great one from Sunkist that catches the seeds and keeps the juice in a little container on the bottom. There are stainless steel ones like this available for about $20.

Measuring cups and spoons
I like 2-cup glass measuring cups which are great for measuring liquids like broth, soy milk, etc.
It is convenient to have at least two sets of dry measuring cups so that you do not always have to wash up before moving to a next step in a recipe.
It is also convenient to have at least two sets of measuring spoons.

Misto pump spray for oils
The Misto brand pump spray allows you to put whatever oil you like in the container and pump the top a few times before getting a spray of oil without fluorocarbons or chemicals. Buy a couple and label one as olive oil for spraying skillets for savory cooking; label the other as canola or another flavorless oil for spraying baking sheets and muffin tins.

Non-stick pan (Le Creuset)
Teflon non-stick pans fall apart in very little time and allow pieces of the coating to get into your food. I think I was buying a new one every year. I do, however, like a non-stick pan to allow for cooking with reduced amounts of oil. I spent a lot of money on Le Creuset which is a very heavy (7 lbs!) cast iron pan with an enamel coating. It works quite well as a non-stick pan, washes well, can go from stove to oven, and has a lifetime guarantee. If I add up the amount I've spent on Teflon pans which were thrown away, I could have bought two Le Creuset!

Sifter for flour
I have a wonderful old one with a handle that turns which I got from my husband's grandmother. You can get a tin hand-cranked flour sifter from Lehman's (www.lehmans.com), a company that makes non-electric old style products, for $21.95.

Wide mouth jars for storing gluten-free flour mixes
This type of jar is readily available at many stores.

Wire whisk
Regular size for making gluten-free flour mixes and lots of other things.
Mini size, like you would use for cocktails, for stirring sauces and salad dressings.

Wok
Great for stir frying large quantities of vegetables or making risotto.

Tools You Can Use

<u>Zester, or microplane grater</u>
Useful for eliminating the stringy pieces while finely grating ginger, or for grating lemon and orange zest.

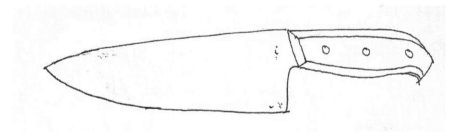

Knife's Lessons

Using a knife properly is one of the most important things you can learn in a kitchen. Not only does proper knife technique prevent injury, *it saves time!* When vegetarians prepare a meal it usually involves a lot of chopping and slicing, so knowing some quick knife techniques will speed your meal prep time. I am not an expert at this, but I have learned a few things from watching chefs, and from macrobiotic cookbooks which promote differently shaped vegetables as part of the Yin-Yang theory. Mostly I have learned knife techniques from my father, a professional-amateur gourmet, who insisted on using the right knife for each job, and for keeping knives properly sharpened. He also tried to teach me to cut straight, which I still cannot do.

<u>Here are my top 11 knife's lessons</u>

1. Purchase good knives and a sharpener,
   > and keep the knives sharp:
   > Use this test before slicing a tomato: can the knife slice a piece of paper?

2. Use the right knife for the job:
   > Most jobs require a good slicing knife which can also be used for small chopping jobs like mincing garlic, ginger, or nuts.
   > A bread knife is a great tool for slicing breads and that is about all.
   > A paring knife is used to peel fruits like apples and pears.
   > A large serrated knife can be used to cut hard vegetables like butternut squash, pumpkin, and potatoes.
   > Use the slicing knife to thinly slice vegetables, julienne, and mince.
   > I find a grapefruit knife a great tool for peeling kiwi, mangoes and other curved fruits.

A chef's knife is used for chopping and mincing, like nuts and garlic.

3. To julienne:

The easiest way to julienne is to cut $\frac{1}{4}$-inch slices of the vegetable and then cut these into matchsticks. If you cut the vegetable into diagonal slices, your matchsticks will be longer.

4. To dice quickly:

Slice as you would for matchsticks; slice the vegetable into stackable slices. Cut these into matchsticks and slice across the matchsticks into dice.

5. To mince quickly (garlic, fresh ginger):

Cut garlic into thin slices. Cut these into slivers. Cut the slivers cross-wise with an up and down motion, placing the weight on the back of the knife.
For ginger, cut a 1-inch piece of ginger and peel it. Cut thin slices of the ginger then cut these into slivers. Cut the slivers cross-wise.

6. Cut on the open side of the vegetable (pepper, tomato):

Vegetables slice easier when you slice on the cut side. For peppers, slice off the stem end of the pepper. Using your fingers, pull the seeds and pith out of the inside of the pepper. Slice the pepper into thin or thick strips on the cut side.

7. 3 ways to slice onions:

Half moons

Cut the onion in half horizontally (not stem to stem). Lay a half flat on your cutting board and cut it in two. Slice each quarter into thick half moon slices.

Round whole slices (rings)

Slice off the stem ends of the onion. Slice rings in the same direction, from one stem end to the other.

Diced

Slice off the stem ends of the onion. Cut the onion in half. Slice one of the halves into slices. Stack a few slices at a time and cut crosswise (opposite to the rings) to make a fine dice. Repeat with the other half of the onion.

8. Foods to snip with a scissors instead of a knife:
    Nori sheets, fresh herbs like rosemary and chives

9. Quickly chopping nuts:
    Place a small amount of nuts (up to a half cup) on a cutting board. Use your chef's knife by placing most of the weight towards the back of the knife and bringing the back of the knife up and down in a quick chopping motion.

10. Paper thin slices:
    The only trick to this is having a really sharp slicing knife. If it is sharp enough to slice paper, then it can make paper-thin slices of tomato.

11. Peeling and slicing citrus fruits:
    Slice off the two ends of the fruit. Score the peel vertically from one end to the other and make several of these cuts. Use your fingers to pull the peel from the fruit.

MUFFINS, PANCAKES and WAFFLES

Muffin and Pancake Baking Tips

We have had a long-standing tradition in my home of eating fresh eggs and home-baked muffins on Sunday mornings. In the past, I emphasized whole grains and reduced fat and sugar. Creating recipes that are both gluten-free and use only unrefined sugars poses a challenge but I've developed a formula for the basic muffin to which many possibilities for variations may be added.

Although we work hard in my home to reduce paper waste, I have found that paper cupcake liners work very well with muffins, but spraying your muffin tin with cooking spray or brushing the tin lightly with oil will work also. I especially like unbleached paper baking cups. If you do use the paper liners, these must be sprayed with oil to allow for easy removal from the muffins when ready to eat.

The natural foods stores sell cooking spray with non-fluorocarbon propellant; however, these still have chemicals. You can also purchase a refillable pump spray and label it with the type of oil inside. Alternatively, you can use a pastry brush and brush oil into each muffin cup.

Most of my muffin recipes make 12 muffins. Once you've gone to the effort of baking muffins, put a few in a ziploc bag to be eaten within a day or two and freeze the rest. Freeze the muffins in easy-to-open-and-close zipper bags, preferably the heavier freezer type. Label the outside with the type of muffin and the date. You should label the bag with all food restrictions, for example: gluten-free, casein-free, no refined sugar.

Defrost a few muffins at a time by placing frozen ones in another bag or tin and allowing them to come to room temperature. Gluten-free muffins taste best when re-warmed in the oven. Warm the muffins at 350° for 5 minutes.

Gluten-free Flour Mixes
I keep two different gluten-free flour mixes on hand all the time and I keep a label inside the jar with the recipe. This way it is easy to replenish my supply without having to take out a cookbook, and I always know which flour mix is which.

Rice Flour Mix
makes 5 cups
4 cups rice flour (I like the texture of superfine white rice or superfine brown rice flour from Authentic Foods)
1 cup potato starch
1 cup tapioca flour

In a dry sifter, place all ingredients for the flour mix. Sift mixture into a large bowl. Spoon flour mix back into sifter and sift again. Sift a third time. Give the mix a final stir with a wire whisk and then spoon it into a wide-mouth jar or container with an air-tight lid.

Sorghum-Millet Flour Mix
makes 5 cups
1 cup sorghum flour (Authentic Foods has a superfine sorghum flour)
$1\frac{1}{2}$ cup tapioca flour (tapioca starch)
$1\frac{1}{2}$ cup potato starch (not potato flour)
1 cup millet flour (or corn flour)

In a dry sifter, place all ingredients for the flour mix. Sift mixture into a large bowl. Spoon flour mix back into sifter and sift again. Sift a third time. Give the mix a final stir with a wire whisk and then spoon it into a wide-mouth jar or container with an air-tight lid.

Apple Spice Muffins
Makes 12 muffins

These apple-spice muffins contain no eggs and are relatively low in fat with only two tablespoons of oil. The molasses adds a nice dark color but if you are not fond of molasses use an additional tablespoon of maple syrup. Feel free to add $\frac{1}{4}$ cup chopped pecans or walnuts.

Dry ingredients
1$\frac{3}{4}$ cup gluten-free flour mix
$\frac{1}{2}$ tsp baking soda
1$\frac{1}{2}$ tsp xanthan gum
1 Tbsp baking powder
$\frac{1}{4}$ tsp salt
$\frac{1}{4}$ tsp nutmeg
$\frac{1}{2}$ tsp cinnamon
1/8 tsp each, ginger and cloves

Wet ingredients
$\frac{1}{4}$ cup maple syrup
1 Tbsp molasses (or maple syrup)
2 Tbsp canola oil
1 Tbsp apple cider vinegar
$\frac{1}{4}$ cup apple juice or cider
$\frac{1}{2}$ cup plain soymilk
1 tsp vanilla
1 cup peeled, chopped apple

Preheat oven to 400°. Combine dry ingredients in a large bowl.
Combine wet ingredients in a medium-sized bowl.
Add wet ingredients to the dry and stir until combined.
Spoon batter equally into lightly oiled muffin cups.
Bake 15-20 minutes until lightly browned and a toothpick inserted into the center comes out clean.

Banana Date Nut Muffins
Makes 12 muffins

These muffins will work with 1 or 2 eggs. If you are not vegan or allergic to eggs use the two as this makes a lighter muffin. If you wish to omit eggs, use an egg replacement to substitute for **one** egg and don't worry about the other. Thawed frozen bananas will work just as well as fresh.

Dry ingredients
1¾ cup gluten-free flour mix
1½ tsp xanthan gum
1 Tbsp baking powder
¼ tsp salt
¼ tsp nutmeg
½ tsp cinnamon
Zest of 1 lemon
1/3 cup chopped dates (flour free)
1/3 cup chopped pecans

Wet ingredients
2-3 ripe bananas, mashed
2 eggs
1/3 cup canola oil
1/3 cup maple syrup
½ cup plain soymilk
1 tsp vanilla

Preheat oven to 400°.
Combine dry ingredients in medium-sized bowl.
Combine wet ingredients in a small bowl.
Add wet ingredients to dry and stir until well combined.
Line muffin tin with paper muffin cups and oil them with cooking spray, or you can just oil the muffin tin without the paper liners.
Divide batter equally into muffin cups.
Bake 15-20 minutes until tops of muffins are firm.

Carrot Cake Muffins
12 muffins

Carrot cake is one of my favorite desserts and I have it every year on my birthday. These muffins really do taste like carrot cake, but without all that sugar and fat. Yum!

1¾ cups gluten-free flour mix
¼ cup teff flour
2 tsp baking soda
1 tsp xanthan gum
2 tsp cinnamon
½ cup shredded, unsweetened coconut
½ cup raisins
½ cup chopped pecans
2 cups grated carrot
½ cup maple syrup
½ cup apple juice
1 Tbsp apple cider vinegar
1/3 cup canola oil
1/3 cup unsweetened applesauce
1 tsp vanilla

Preheat oven to 350°.
Lightly oil muffin tin or line with unbleached paper liners.
In a large bowl, combine the gluten-free flour mix, teff flour, baking soda, xanthan gum, cinnamon, coconut, raisins, pecans and carrot.
Toss with a fork until combined.
In a medium bowl, combine maple syrup, apple juice, cider vinegar, oil, applesauce, and vanilla.
Add the wet ingredients to the dry and stir to combine.
Spoon batter into muffin cups.
Bake 30-35 minutes. Tops will be lightly browned and a toothpick inserted into a muffin will come out clean.

Cranberry Orange Muffins
Makes 12 muffins

Cranberries paired with orange reminds me of autumn and Thanksgiving. But I love the tangy taste of cranberries so much that I buy several packages to freeze for when they are no longer in season so I can enjoy them all year. To make these muffins vegan, use a replacement for the egg and maple syrup or agave nectar instead of the honey.

$1\frac{3}{4}$ cup gluten-free flour mix
$1\frac{1}{2}$ tsp xanthan gum
1 Tbsp baking powder
$\frac{1}{2}$ tsp baking soda
2 Tbsp canola oil
1 egg
$\frac{1}{4}$ cup apple juice or orange juice
$\frac{1}{2}$ cup plain soymilk
$\frac{1}{2}$ tsp vanilla
$\frac{1}{4}$ cup honey
$\frac{3}{4}$ cup whole fresh cranberries, finely chopped in a food processor
Grated peel of whole orange (wash first)
Optional: add chopped walnuts (1/4 c)

Preheat oven to 400°.
Lightly oil muffin tin or line with paper liners and lightly oil the papers.
In a large bowl place gluten-free flour mix, xanthan gum, and baking powder.
Add orange peel and cranberries and toss with a fork until combined.
In a smaller bowl combine canola oil, egg, apple juice, soymilk, vanilla, and honey.
Add the wet ingredients to the dry and stir lightly to combine. Do not overmix.
Fill muffin cups $\frac{1}{2}$ full and then add more to each cup until all batter is used. Bake for 15-20 minutes.

Cranberry Pear Ginger Muffins
Makes 12 muffins

Cranberries and pears are autumn fruits so this is definitely an autumn muffin. Buy fresh cranberries when they are in season and freeze them right in their bags. When using cranberries in muffins, chop or halve fresh or frozen cranberries. Defrosting frozen cranberries makes them a little mushy which is fine for a crisp or sautéed fruit, but not for baked goods. To make these vegan use an egg replacement and fruit juice concentrate or Agave nectar instead of the honey.

$\frac{3}{4}$ cup chopped or halved fresh cranberries
$\frac{3}{4}$ cup peeled, diced firm but ripe pear (Bosc or Anjou)
1 tsp minced fresh ginger
$1\frac{3}{4}$ cup gluten-free flour mix
1 Tbsp baking powder
$\frac{3}{4}$ tsp ground ginger
1 tsp xanthan gum
1 egg
$\frac{1}{2}$ cup plain soymilk
$\frac{1}{4}$ cup canola oil
$\frac{1}{4}$ cup honey or agave nectar
$\frac{1}{4}$ cup maple syrup
1 tsp vanilla

Oil a 12-cup muffin tin and pre-heat oven to 400°.
Chop cranberries and pear and place in small bowl.
Add minced ginger and set aside.
In a large bowl combine gluten-free flour mix, baking powder, ground ginger, and xanthan gum.
In a medium bowl combine the egg, soymilk, oil, honey, maple syrup, and vanilla.
Add wet ingredients to dry ingredients and gently stir until just combined.
Stir in cranberries, pear, and fresh ginger.
Divide batter equally into muffin cups.
Bake for 20 minutes.

Crunchy Millet Muffins
Makes 12

The original of this recipe is a favorite of my friend Betsy and her cycling buddies. I changed several ingredients to make them gluten-free and a little healthier, reducing both the fat and sugar. The result is a lovely yellow muffin with a delightful crunch.

1 cup millet, uncooked
$\frac{1}{2}$ cup millet flour
$\frac{1}{2}$ cup sorghum flour
2/3 cup potato starch
1/3 cup tapioca starch
$1\frac{1}{2}$ tsp aluminum-free baking powder
$\frac{1}{2}$ tsp baking soda
1 tsp xanthan gum
$\frac{1}{2}$ tsp sea salt
1 Tbsp vanilla
$\frac{1}{4}$ tsp almond extract
$\frac{1}{2}$ cup soymilk or rice milk
2 eggs
$\frac{1}{2}$ cup canola oil
$\frac{1}{2}$ cup pure maple syrup
1 Tbsp cider vinegar

Preheat oven to 375°.
Toast millet in a dry skillet over medium heat until fragrant and beginning to pop. Remove from heat and cool.
In a large bowl combine millet flour, sorghum flour, potato starch, and tapioca starch. Use a wire whisk to combine thoroughly.
Add baking powder, baking soda, xanthan gum, and sea salt and whisk to combine. Stir in cooled, toasted millet.
In a small bowl, lightly beat eggs, then add the canola oil, vanilla, soymilk, and maple syrup. Stir to combine.
Add the wet ingredients to the dry and stir to combine.
Spoon the batter into lightly oiled muffin cups and bake for 20-25 minutes.

Gingerbread Muffins
Makes 8-10 muffins

This batter is very sticky and gooey. Replace the egg with egg substitute to make vegan muffins.

Dry ingredients
$1\frac{3}{4}$ cup gluten-free flour mix
$1\frac{1}{2}$ tsp xanthan gum
1 Tbsp baking powder
$\frac{1}{4}$ tsp baking soda
$\frac{3}{4}$ tsp cinnamon
$\frac{3}{4}$ tsp ginger
$\frac{1}{4}$ tsp cloves

Wet ingredients
$\frac{1}{4}$ cup Blackstrap molasses
2 Tbsp maple syrup
1 egg, lightly beaten
1/3 cup canola oil
$\frac{1}{4}$ cup plain soymilk
1 tsp cider vinegar

Preheat oven to 400°.
Combine dry ingredients in medium-sized bowl.
Combine wet ingredients in a small bowl.
Add wet ingredients to dry and stir until well combined.
Line muffin tin with paper muffin cups and oil them with cooking spray.
Divide batter equally into muffin cups.
Bake 15-20 minutes until tops of muffins are firm.

Maple Corn Muffins
Makes 12 muffins

Variation: use blue cornmeal (Arrowhead Mills or other brand) and add ½ cup frozen blueberries and increase maple syrup to ¼ cup. I especially like the organic wild blueberries which are very small. To make these vegan, use an egg substitute to replace the egg.

Dry ingredients
1 cup cornmeal
1 cup gluten-free flour mix
1 Tbsp baking powder
1 ½ tsp xanthan gum

Wet ingredients
1 egg
1 cup plain soy milk
¼ cup canola oil
2 Tbsp pure maple syrup
½ tsp vanilla

Preheat oven to 400°.
Mix together dry ingredients in a large bowl.
Mix wet ingredients in a smaller bowl.
Add wet ingredients to the dry and stir until combined.
Use cupcake papers to line the muffin tin and spray these with canola oil cooking spray. Or you can oil the muffin tin and not use paper liners.
Fill muffin cups ½ to 2/3 full, dividing the batter evenly amongst the cups.
Bake 15 -20 min. until lightly browned and a toothpick inserted into the center comes out clean.

Pineapple Coconut Muffins
12 muffins

Or shall we say piña colada? I think these muffins are my favorite in the book. They are simply delicious! For a vegan muffin (or egg allergy) omit the egg and add ¼ cup unsweetened applesauce to help bind them; the combination of baking soda and citrus will raise the muffins.

1¾ cup gluten-free flour mix
1½ tsp xanthan gum
1 Tbsp baking powder
½ tsp baking soda
¼ tsp nutmeg
1/3 cup shredded, unsweetened coconut (Let's Do Organic)
1/3 cup chopped pecans
2/3 cup drained crushed pineapple
1 egg, lightly beaten
1/3 cup canola oil
¼ cup frozen orange juice concentrate (undiluted), thawed
1 tsp vanilla
1/3 cup maple syrup

Preheat oven to 400°.
In a large bowl, stir together gluten-free flour mix, xanthan gum, baking powder, baking soda, nutmeg, coconut, and pecans.
In a medium bowl, mix with a fork the pineapple, egg, oil, orange juice concentrate, vanilla, and maple syrup.
Add the wet ingredients to the dry and stir gently until fully mixed together.
Spoon the batter into greased muffin tins or lightly oiled paper liners.
Bake 15-20 minutes.

Pumpkin Muffins
Makes 12 muffins

These muffins, sweetened with maple syrup and date puree, are very moist and spicy, with a streusel topping of nuts or pumpkin seeds, maple sugar, and cinnamon. An added benefit: pumpkin seeds are alkalizing to the body.

Dry ingredients

2 cups gluten-free flour mix
1 ½ tsp xanthan gum
1 Tbsp baking powder
½ tsp cinnamon
½ tsp nutmeg

¼ tsp each cloves, ginger, allspice
¼ tsp sea salt

Wet ingredients

1 egg
¾ cup pumpkin puree
2/3 cup plain soy milk
¼ cup maple syrup
¼ cup date puree or applesauce
2 Tbsp agave nectar
¼ cup canola oil

Topping

2 Tbsp ground nuts (pecans, almonds, pumpkin seeds)
2 Tbsp maple sugar
1 tsp cinnamon

Preheat oven to 400°.
Lightly oil a muffin tin or line with paper liners and spray these with oil.
In a large mixing bowl, combine the gluten-free flour mix, xanthan gum, baking powder, spices, and salt.
In a medium sized bowl, combine the egg, pumpkin, soy milk, maple syrup, date puree, and oil. Stir until combined.
In a small bowl, stir together the pumpkin seeds, maple sugar, and 1 tsp cinnamon.
Add the wet ingredients to the dry and combine thoroughly.
Spoon the batter evenly into muffin cups.
Using a tablespoon, sprinkle the streusel topping on the muffins.
Bake the muffins for 20 minutes.
Freeze any muffins you don't use.

Pumpkin Pancakes
Makes about 12 medium-sized pancakes

I make these pancakes when I have leftover pumpkin from a large can. They are light and puff up if you make them small, about 2 inches across, and with a hint of cinnamon they smell so good while they're cooking. Once, I was halfway through making the batter and realized that I had no pumpkin. I substituted unsweetened applesauce with delicious results. To make vegan pancakes use an egg replacement. Serve with juice-sweetened apple butter or mix some date or maple sugar with cinnamon and sprinkle on the pancakes.

Dry ingredients
1 cup gluten-free flour mix
2 tsp aluminum-free baking powder
$\frac{1}{4}$ tsp cinnamon
$\frac{1}{2}$ tsp xanthan gum
$\frac{1}{4}$ tsp baking soda

Wet ingredients
1 egg
1 Tbsp oil
$\frac{1}{2}$ cup canned pumpkin puree
        (or applesauce)
$\frac{1}{2}$ cup plain soymilk
1 Tbsp maple syrup

Mix dry ingredients into a medium bowl.
Combine wet ingredients in a bowl and add to the dry ingredients. Stir to combine.
If the batter seems thick, thin with more soy milk 1 Tbsp at a time.
Cook pancakes.

Lemon Poppyseed Muffins
Makes 12

These muffins are lemony and poppyseedy with a lovely glaze made of freshly squeezed lemon juice and agave nectar. They are one of my favorite muffins!

Dry ingredients
¾ cup garbanzo flour
¼ cup potato starch flour
¼ cup tapioca starch
¼ cup rice flour (preferably superfine white or brown)
½ tsp xanthan gum
¾ tsp baking soda
1 tsp baking powder
¼ tsp sea salt
3 Tbsp poppyseeds
Grated rind of 1 lemon

Wet ingredients
1 egg, lightly beaten
¼ cup canola oil
1 6-oz container of plain soy yogurt
1 tsp vanilla extract
¼ tsp lemon extract
½ cup agave nectar

Glaze
2 Tbsp fresh lemon juice
1 Tbsp + 1 tsp agave nectar
Grated rind of ½ lemon

Preheat oven to 350°.
Lightly oil muffin cups.
In a large bowl, combine the dry ingredients.
In a medium bowl, combine the wet ingredients.
Add the wet ingredients to the dry and fold together until combined.
Fill muffin cups about ½ full.

Bake for 15-17 minutes, until lightly browned and a toothpick inserted into the center comes out clean.

While muffins bake, prepare glaze; combine all ingredients and whisk together.

Remove muffin tin from oven and place on cooling rack. While muffins are still hot, poke about four holes in each using a toothpick.

Spoon the glaze over the muffins, ½ tsp at a time. Allow the glaze to soak into each muffin. Don't worry if the glaze runs over the edge of the muffin tin.

Cool the muffins in the pan. Do not be impatient, this is very important.

Once cooled, remove the muffins from the pan and enjoy!

Buckwheat Pancakes

Makes about 12 pancakes, about 3-4 inch diameter

The batter is very sticky and requires that you smooth it out after dropping it in the pan. The buckwheat has a wonderful earthy taste and the pancakes are especially delicious with Spiced Dried Apples (see Pancake and Waffle Toppings) or serve with warm maple syrup or sautéed fruit with cinnamon. To make this vegan, replace or omit egg.

<u>Dry Ingredients</u>
¾ cup buckwheat flour
¾ cup gluten-free flour mix
1½ tsp baking powder
½ tsp baking soda
½ tsp xanthan gum

<u>Wet Ingredients</u>
1 egg + 1 egg white
1 1/3 cup soymilk
1 Tbsp canola oil
1 tsp vanilla

Combine dry ingredients in a large bowl.
Combine wet ingredients in a small bowl.
Add wet ingredients to dry and combine thoroughly.
Make pancakes as usual.

Cornmeal Pancakes
Makes about 12 4-inch pancakes

These pancakes have a delicious real corn taste. If you find the color of the pancakes made by the molasses to be unpleasing, you can use maple syrup, agave nectar, or no sweetener at all. Years ago, on the Navajo reservation in Arizona, we ate blue cornmeal pancakes and have enjoyed this alternative ever since. Arrowhead Mills makes a blue cornmeal which I have found at Whole Foods markets. The maple syrup sweetener with the blue cornmeal makes a more appealing color, allowing the "blue" color to remain. Or for a very "blue" meal serve with a blueberry fruit sauce: warm some fresh or frozen blueberries sweetened with honey, agave nectar, or fruit juice concentrate, until the blueberries pop and a sauce is formed. Thicken the sauce with some kuzu powder or arrowroot powder; dissolve 1-2 tsp powder in 1 Tbsp warm water and add to the sauce.

$\frac{3}{4}$ cup cornmeal
$\frac{3}{4}$ cup gluten-free flour mix
$\frac{3}{4}$ tsp xanthan gum
1 Tbsp baking powder
1 egg
1$\frac{1}{4}$ cup soymilk
1 Tbsp canola oil
1 Tbsp molasses or maple syrup

Mix all ingredients together.
Using a griddle or skillet oiled with canola oil or spray, cook pancakes over medium heat.
Serve hot with warm maple syrup or blueberry sauce.

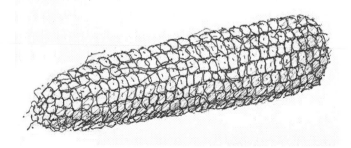

Cornmeal Waffles, Plain and Lemon Rosemary
Make 12 waffles

This recipe makes very crispy waffles that are delicious with pure maple syrup or unsweetened apple butter. If you have any leftovers, pack them in a large Ziploc bag (for easy access), label and freeze. To use frozen waffles, toast them in a toaster or toaster oven just as you would store-bought frozen waffles. For a special occasion breakfast, try my Lemon-Rosemary variation.

2 eggs
$1\frac{3}{4}$ cup plain soy milk
6 Tbsp canola oil
1 Tbsp maple syrup
$1\frac{1}{2}$ cup cornmeal
$\frac{1}{2}$ cup gluten-free flour mix
4 tsp aluminum-free baking powder
$\frac{1}{2}$ tsp sea salt
$\frac{1}{2}$ tsp xanthan gum

Combine eggs, soy milk, oil, and maple syrup in a small bowl.
In a large bowl combine cornmeal, gluten-free flour mix, baking powder, sea salt, and xanthan gum.
Add wet ingredients to the dry and mix well.
Proceed with cooking the batter on a waffle iron according to the manufacturer's instructions for your particular waffle iron.

Variation
Lemon Rosemary Cornmeal Waffles
Make the recipe as above but use 1 cup cornmeal and 1 cup gluten-free flour mix (instead of $1\frac{1}{2}$ cup cornmeal and $\frac{1}{2}$ cup flour mix)
Add grated lemon zest of 1 lemon and 1 Tbsp minced fresh rosemary.

Lemon Syrup
Melt together 1 Tbsp ghee, 3 Tbsp honey, and 2 Tbsp fresh lemon juice. Use this syrup over the waffles.

Pancake and Waffle Toppings

In addition to pure maple syrup and all fruit jam, here are some pancake and waffle toppings that will make your pancake and waffle breakfast much more interesting and nutritious. Use berries when in season and dried apples or lemon syrup in the winter.

<u>Spiced Dried Apples</u>
makes 2 cups
1½ cups apple juice or orange juice
2 cups dried, unsweetened, unsulfured apples, chopped
½ tsp cinnamon
¼ tsp cloves
1-2 Tbsp maple syrup (optional)

Combine the juice, apples, maple syrup if using, and spices in a small saucepan and cook over low heat until apples are very soft and half of the liquid has been absorbed.

<u>Berry Syrup</u>
1 cup berries in season (blueberries, strawberries, or raspberries)
2-4 Tbsp maple syrup
Grated lemon or orange rind if desired

Combine the berries and syrup in a small saucepan and cook over low heat until the berries burst and become a sauce.

<u>Lemon Syrup</u>
Melt together 1 Tbsp ghee, 3 Tbsp honey or agave nectar, and 2 Tbsp fresh lemon juice.

<u>Sautéed Fruit</u>
See *Desserts* for recipe.

<u>Apple Butter</u>
Juice-sweetened apple butter (I like McCutcheon's).

Mom's Fruit Compote
See *Snacks* for recipe.

Cinnamon Sugar
Combine 2 Tbsp maple or date sugar with 1 tsp cinnamon and 2
Tbsp finely chopped pecans or walnuts (nuts are optional).

Multigrain Oat Pancakes
Makes 12 4-inch pancakes

Gluten-free oats has opened up a world of possibilities! We
love the chewy texture of these oat pancakes. For variation,
add a $\frac{1}{2}$ tsp ground cinnamon to the batter. Serve them up with
some juice-sweetened apple butter for a delicious, filling, high
fiber breakfast.

$\frac{3}{4}$ cup gluten-free flour mix
2 Tbsp teff flour
2 Tbsp cornmeal
$\frac{1}{2}$ cup gluten-free rolled oats
1 Tbsp baking powder
$\frac{1}{4}$ tsp sea salt
1 Tbsp ground flax
1 cup plain soymilk
1 egg
1 Tbsp canola or vegetable oil
1 tsp agave nectar
1 tsp vanilla

Combine oats and soymilk in a medium bowl and let soak for 15
minutes. In another bowl, whisk together the gluten-free flour
mix, teff flour, cornmeal, baking powder, sea salt, and flax.
After the 15 minute soaking, add the egg, oil, vanilla, and agave
nectar to the oat-soymilk mixture.
Add the oat mixture to the dry ingredients and stir until fully
combined.
Proceed with pancake making!

Pumpkin Pecan Waffles
Makes 12 waffles

I love just about anything with pumpkin. These waffles are scrumptious with the "pumpkin pie spices" and the pecan finish. The nuts are optional but really add something special. Make sure the nuts are finely chopped or they will make closing the waffle iron more difficult. Serve with sautéed apples or spicy fruit-sweetened apple butter. Label and freeze any that are not eaten the day you make them.

2 cups gluten-free flour mix
1 Tbsp baking powder
1½ tsp xanthan gum
¼ tsp each cinnamon, nutmeg, ginger
1/8 tsp allspice
¼ tsp sea salt
½ cup oil
2 eggs
¾ cup pumpkin puree
1¾ cup plain soy milk
1 Tbsp maple syrup
¼ cup finely chopped pecans (optional but delicious!)

Prepare and heat waffle iron according to manufacturer's instructions.
Combine the gluten-free flour mix, baking powder, xanthan gum, spices, and salt in a large mixing bowl.
Combine oil, eggs, pumpkin, soy milk and maple syrup in a medium sized bowl.
Add the wet ingredients to the dry and stir to mix well. Add more soy milk or orange juice to thin the batter if necessary. If using the pecans, add them here.
Cook the waffles according to your particular waffle iron instructions.
Keep the cooked waffles warm in an oven set to 300°, using the oven racks to keep the waffles crisp.

Side Salads and Soups

Making Your Own Vegetable Broth

I learned early on in the gluten free journey that many
commercially prepared broths contain wheat gluten. There are
gluten-free and organic versions available in natural foods
stores but they are expensive if you are using them on a
regular basis. I use a lot of vegetable broth in soups and
risotto which would be quite an expense as well as a lot of
pantry space if I did not make my own. When I make broth I
divide it into several containers of different sizes and freeze
it; this way I always have a stash of broth on hand.

I do not buy vegetables for the purpose of making broth; I
save the tops and peelings of washed vegetables and use these.
During the week as you are preparing various meals, wash your
vegetables before cutting and peeling. Save the tops (no dirt),
bottoms, peels, skins; save anything that you would discard or
compost except rotten or mushy parts. Keep these peelings in
a plastic bag or container for no longer than three days,
preferably in a vegetable crisper.

When you are ready to make the broth, put all the peelings,
tops, and bottoms in a soup pot and add enough water to cover.
The vegetables will rise to the surface and float; push them
down with a slotted spoon. Bring to a boil and then turn down
heat and simmer for about 30 minutes. The broth will be a
beautiful orange color and have a pleasant vegetable odor.
Strain the broth over a large bowl or container, removing the
cooked vegetables. Discard the vegetables, and cool the broth
before pouring into freezer containers.

Side Salads and Soups

To defrost broth run very hot water over the freezer container until the frozen mass of broth loosens from the sides. Empty the still-frozen broth into a saucepan and heat until melted.

See the list below for good choices of vegetables to use for broth. Always include some onion skins as these contribute a wonderful orange color.

<u>Good for broth</u>
Celery tops and bottoms
Onion skins (not red)
Onions (not red)
Carrot peelings, ends
Fresh ginger, the peel and ends that you would discard
Small amount garlic (garlic can overpower the flavor if you use too much)
Tops, bottoms, and peelings of parsnip, turnip, and rutabaga
Zucchini tops and bottoms
Butternut squash tops and peels
Green beans
Fresh parsley, basil, rosemary, cilantro

<u>Do Not Use</u>
Beets, cabbage, broccoli, cauliflower, or asparagus

Broccoli Stem Salad
Serves 4

Ever feel guilty about throwing away those broccoli stems and wonder if there was something other than compost that could be done with them? There is! This salad of raw matchstick broccoli stems is surprisingly delicious with the Mediterranean combination of flavors, garlic and lemon juice. Broccoli stems are high in vitamin C and phytonutrients.

$1\frac{1}{2}$ lbs broccoli stems
2 plum tomatoes, chopped
1 clove garlic, minced
$\frac{1}{4}$ tsp sea salt
2 tsp lemon juice
1 tsp red wine vinegar
$1\frac{1}{2}$ Tbsp olive oil
Freshly ground pepper
Pine nuts (optional)

Peel the broccoli stems using a paring knife. Slice the stems lengthwise into 1/8 inch width slices. Stack a couple of the long slices and cut into matchsticks. Place the broccoli strips in a medium sized bowl.
Add the chopped tomatoes.
Combine the garlic with salt in a small bowl.
Add the lemon juice, vinegar, and olive oil and stir to combine. Pour this dressing over the salad and toss with a fork to combine.
Grind pepper over the salad to your taste.
Season with more salt if needed.

You may want to garnish the salad with pine nuts.

Basic Miso Soup
Serves 1 or 2, easily multiplied

Sometimes I just feel like having some soup for lunch on a cold day and I have nothing prepared. What I love about miso soup, in addition to its health benefits, is that it can be made with no forethought and I tend to have all of the ingredients available. Instant soup! I have experimented a lot with making miso soup and this is my basic recipe which I find flavorful and not too overpowering with miso. Miso is already a fermented product so it keeps for a long time in the refrigerator. The seasoning ingredients and sea vegetables are pantry items, and the tofu is vacuum-packed, so it is easy to always have these ingredients on hand. I discuss the health benefits of miso in the *Good Nutrition Tips for Healthy Vegetarians* section of the book. This makes a large serving for one person, or a 1 cup serving for two people.

2 cups water
2 inch piece of Kombu sea vegetable
2 mushrooms, sliced
2 scallions, sliced
4 tsp mellow rice miso
$\frac{1}{2}$ tsp grated ginger
1 tsp mirin (rice wine)
2 tsp wheat-free soy sauce or tamari
2 oz firm silken tofu, vacuum-packed works well for this, cut into tiny cubes
1 tsp Wakame Instant sea vegetable
$\frac{1}{2}$ tsp sesame oil
Optional additions: handful fresh spinach sliced into ribbons, $\frac{1}{4}$ cup grated carrot, leftover 100% buckwheat soba noodles.

Bring the two cups of water and the Kombu to a boil. Turn down heat to simmer and continue cooking for 4 minutes. Remove Kombu and turn heat to low.
Add mushrooms and scallions to your broth and continue to cook over very low flame.

In a small dish place the miso and add a few Tbsp of the hot broth. Mix these together by mushing the miso with the back of a spoon until dissolved. A mini wire whisk is a great tool for dissolving the miso.

Add the dissolved miso into the soup.

Add the grated ginger, mirin, wheat-free soy sauce, tofu, and wakame.

Add any of the optional additions or finish the soup with the sesame oil.

Blueberry Spinach Salad

This recipe was given to me by Annemarie McGeady, a fellow swim team parent. The original had blue cheese sprinkled on the salad. The recipe makes a lot of dressing which you will have left over for more delicious salads after this one is gone.

Package of baby spinach
2 cups fresh blueberries
½ cup chopped, toasted pecans

Dressing
1 shallot
1 cup fresh blueberries
1 tsp salt
3 Tbsp pure maple syrup or 2 Tbsp agave nectar
½ cup raspberry vinegar
1 cup canola oil

Toss salad ingredients in large serving bowl.

For dressing, whirl shallot and blueberries in food processor until pureed and place in medium bowl. Add rest of dressing ingredients and stir.

Serve salad with dressing on the side.

Carrot Soup
6 large first course servings

Although there are lots of spices and flavorings that would make carrot soup unusual, I like mine unadulterated, just vegetables and broth pureed with a dash of salt and pepper. This soup tastes very rich if you use the ghee as suggested, and turns out a very rich orange color as well.

1 lb carrots
1 fist-sized potato (Russet, Yukon Gold, or White)
$\frac{1}{2}$ onion
1 medium shallot
1 Tbsp ghee (or olive oil)
6 cups water
1 bay leaf
Sea salt and freshly ground pepper to season

Peel carrots and cut into chunks.
Peel potato and cut into quarters.
Slice onion and shallot.
In saucepan sauté onion and shallot in ghee or olive oil.
Add carrots, potato, water, and bay leaf.
Bring to a boil, then turn down heat to medium.
Simmer covered about 20-30 minutes, until carrots and potato are soft enough to pierce with a fork.
Remove bay leaf.
Wait until cool, then puree in blender or food processor.
Season with salt and pepper to taste.
Return to the pot and reheat gently.

Celeriac Soup
Serves 4 as a first course

Celeriac, pronounced sell-er-ee-ak, also known as celery knob, is a large root which appears rather ugly before you pare off the hairy roots to its creamy white center. Used a lot in French cooking, it imparts a celery flavor which is fairly strong when eaten raw but much milder when cooked, as in this soup. Celeriac is great paired with tart apples, grated and eaten raw in salads, mashed with potatoes, or added to soup. This soup is very creamy even thought it has no dairy, and if you have never experienced celeriac then I am excited to introduce you to it.

1 Tbsp ghee and 1 Tbsp olive oil
1 medium onion, chopped
1 stalk celery, sliced
1 clove garlic, minced
1 shallot, thinly sliced
1 lb celeriac, peeled and cut into large cubes
4 cups vegetable broth
$\frac{1}{2}$ cup plain soy milk (optional)
Sea salt and freshly ground black pepper for seasoning
Fresh parsley, minced, for garnish

In a medium sized soup pot, heat the ghee and oil over medium heat. Cook the onion, celery, garlic and shallot until softened, about 2 minutes.
Add celeriac and vegetable broth and bring to boiling.
Turn heat to low, cover, and simmer about 15-20 minutes, until celeriac is tender.
Puree the soup in a blender and return to soup pot.
Taste the soup and season to your liking with salt and pepper.
You can thin the soup to desired consistency with the soy milk, or with more vegetable broth.
Serve in bowls with about 1-2 tsp minced parsley sprinkled on top.
I must add that the parsley adds a splash of color to a "white" soup, and it imparts a splash of flavor as well.

Composed Salad with Pears and Pecans
Serves 4

I love composed salads. They look beautiful set up on colorful salad plates and allow me to individualize the ingredients to what I have on hand and what each diner likes. Composed salads feel more special, like we are eating in a restaurant. Be creative in how you "compose" your salad with the ingredients I have listed.

4 of your best, most colorful salad plates
4 cups organic spring mix greens
1 bulb fennel or 1 head Belgian endive (not curly)
8 raw mushrooms, washed and dried
8 red radishes
8 grape tomatoes or cherry tomatoes
4 comice or seckle pears, the small ones, or 2 Anjou pears
$\frac{1}{4}$ cup chopped pecans

Raspberry Vinaigrette
$\frac{1}{4}$ cup raspberry vinegar
$\frac{1}{4}$ cup olive oil
1 tsp Dijon mustard
1 shallot

Divide the spring mix greens evenly on the four plates.
Slice the fennel or endive crosswise thinly into 1 inch slices and sprinkle them decoratively over the salad. Do not use the hard core of the endive.
Thinly slice the mushrooms and arrange these decoratively on each salad.
Thinly slice the radishes and arrange these on the salad, allowing two per person.
Halve the tomatoes and place 4 halves on each plate
If using the small pears halve the pears lengthwise and then cut each half into four thin slices allowing a whole pear per person. If using Anjou pears halve the pears and cut each half into 5 thin segments, allowing a half pear per person.

Arrange the pear slices in a star on top of the salad, with the bottom end of the pear slices in the middle of the salad and the thin end almost touching the edge of the plate.
Sprinkle each salad with 1 Tbsp pecans.

To make the vinaigrette, combine all dressing ingredients in a blender and puree until blended. Pour the dressing into a decorative cruet or small "creamer" and pass with a spoon. A couple of spoonfuls of the dressing are enough to impart a wonderful sweet flavor to the salad.

Deli Style Carrot Salad
Makes about 3 cups
This salad tastes a lot like the shredded carrot salad you see in the deli which is loaded with mayonnaise and fat. My version replaces most of the mayo with a homemade tofu sour cream and turns out very creamy.

1 lb carrots peeled and grated (use the food processor if you have one) (or use the pre-shredded carrots that come in a package, equivalent to 1 lb.)
$\frac{1}{2}$ cup dark raisins
2 Tbsp gluten-free or vegan mayo
1/3 cup tofu sour cream (see Dressings and Sauces)
2 tsp white wine vinegar
1 tsp maple syrup or brown rice syrup

Combine carrots and raisins in a serving bowl.
Mix together the rest of the ingredients and toss with carrots and raisins.
Refrigerate a few hours before serving.

Easy Cranberry Relish

Many cranberry relishes and sauces have a whole lot of added sugar. This simple recipe uses dates and apple to sweeten the cranberries. Make sure you use the pulse function on the food processor so your relish is chunky and not mushy. Frozen cranberries can be used with good results. Defrost the cranberries first.

1 cup fresh whole cranberries
10 pitted dates, soaked for 1 hour
$\frac{1}{2}$ orange, seeds removed, peel on
$\frac{1}{2}$ cup walnuts, soaked for 1 hour, then drained and rinsed
1 crisp apple, washed and cored but not peeled, cut into quarters
1 Tbsp raisins

In the bowl of a food processor, place all ingredients.
Use the pulse button to coarsely chop the ingredients. Do not be tempted to hold the *on* button; it will turn your relish into mush.
When desired consistency is reached, transfer to a serving bowl.

<u>Variation</u>
Add some juice-sweetened dried cranberries to the completed relish.

Easy Greek Salad
Serves 4 as a side dish salad

This is one of those salads that is so simple but so delicious. It is inspired by our trip to Greece where we learned that real Greek salad has no lettuce, only large chunks of the vegetables. Of course in Greece, the salad is served with a large chunk of local Feta cheese. This salad is best in the summer when the vegetables are very fresh from your local farmer's market or vegetable stand.

2 cucumbers
1 green pepper
2 beautiful tomatoes
$\frac{1}{2}$ medium red onion
$\frac{1}{4}$ -$\frac{1}{2}$ cup Kalamata olives, whole with or without pits
Oregano, olive oil, red wine vinegar

Peel (if desired) cucumbers.
Slice cucumber in half the long way (take out seeds if they are large) and cut into chunks.
Cut pepper into chunks.
Cut tomato into chunks.
Thinly slice the red onion.
Combine all in a bowl.
Add olives if using.
Sprinkle with desired amount oregano and drizzle with 1 Tbsp olive oil and 2 Tbsp red wine vinegar.

Jersalem Artichoke Soup

Serves 4 as a first course (sadly with no leftovers)

Neither an artichoke, nor from Jerusalem, the Jerusalem Artichoke grows as a root with a lovely yellow sunflower attached, thus the name "sunchokes" which you may have seen in the grocery store. I was introduced to Jerusalem artichokes by Wilma, my mother-in-law, a wonderful gardener, who grows them in her garden both for the beauty of the sunflower as well as the root vegetable below. The sunchokes are sliced onto salads for a crunch, or cooked into a wonderfully sweet pureed soup with a truly unique flavor. Sunchokes provide a small amount of Vitamin C (4 mg per 4 small artichokes) and iron (3.4 mg per 4 small artichokes). Frieda's sells the "sunchokes" in 1 lb packages, and I have only used ¾ lb for this recipe so that you will have a few left over to try on your salad. Unfortunately, I have never seen Jerusalem artichokes at any of the Farmer's Markets that I go to, but keep your eyes open for them, or, if you garden, try growing them yourself as they are best when fresh.

1 Tbsp olive oil
1 shallot, sliced
¾ lb Jerusalem artichokes, washed, unpeeled, cut into chunks
2 cups vegetable broth
½ cup unsweetened soy milk
Salt and freshly ground pepper to taste

In a medium saucepan, heat oil.
Add shallot and cook until softened, about 1 minute.
Add Jerusalem artichokes and broth and bring to a boil.
Reduce heat to simmer, cover, and cook about 15 minutes until artichokes are tender.
When cooled, puree the soup in the blender.
Return the soup to the pot, and add soy milk, and re-heat gently.
Season to taste with salt and freshly ground pepper.

Moroccan Spicy Carrot Salad
Serves 6 as a side salad

This recipe comes from my mother-in-law and is very simple to make. It tastes best after it has had a chance to "marinate" in the dressing and absorb the flavors. When fresh mint is available it is especially delicious but I have made it in the winter with dried mint as well.

$\frac{1}{2}$ lb carrots, peeled and shredded
1/3 cup golden raisins
$\frac{1}{4}$ cup fresh mint or 1-2 Tbsp dried mint
3 Tbsp fresh lemon juice
2 Tbsp olive oil
1 Tbsp honey
$\frac{1}{2}$ tsp cumin
$\frac{1}{4}$ tsp cayenne

In a large serving bowl combine the shredded carrots, golden raisins, and mint.
Combine the lemon juice, olive oil, honey, cumin, and cayenne in a small bowl and stir together with a small whisk.
Pour the dressing over the salad and toss with a fork to distribute the dressing.
Cover and refrigerate for a few hours before serving.

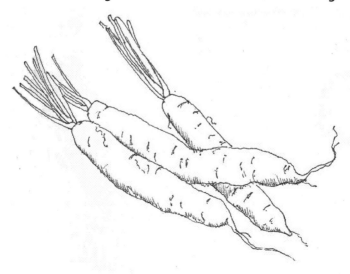

Potato Leek Soup
Serves 4 for dinner with leftovers for lunch

My husband insisted that I include this simple recipe because it is a family favorite. There are few ingredients and it is easy to make. See my instructions on how to clean the leeks so you avoid crunching on sand in your soup. Serve the soup with a colorful salad, and a high protein spread like hummus with some gluten-free crackers or toast.

$1\frac{1}{4}$ lb leeks, sliced (see Note)
$1\frac{1}{2}$ lb potatoes, peeled, and cubed (I like Yukon Gold)
8 cups water
1 Tbsp ghee
1 Tbsp olive oil
1 bay leaf
$\frac{1}{2}$ tsp sea salt
Freshly ground pepper

In a large soup pot, melt the ghee then add the olive oil.
Sauté the leeks over medium heat until coated in the oil and slightly softened.
Add the potatoes and continue to sauté for another minute.
Add the water, bay leaf, and salt.
Bring to a boil then turn the heat down to medium.
Simmer the soup for about 45 minutes, until potatoes are very tender.
Remove bay leaf and add pepper to taste.
Remove about $\frac{1}{2}$ of the soup to a blender or food processor and blend until pureed.
Add the puree back to the soup pot.
Taste the soup and add more salt if necessary.

Note:
To clean the leeks, rinse the outside in lukewarm water and slice off the root ends and about $\frac{1}{2}$ inch of the tops including any part of the top that is mushy or unsightly.
Slice the leeks lengthwise from bottom to top.

Under running lukewarm water, open the outer leaves and with your fingers remove the sand. Do this with the inner layers while keeping the leek somewhat intact so that it can be sliced.

Pumpkin Soup
Serves 4 for dinner

If you don't have a pumpkin you can use a butternut squash. Serve the soup with salad and toasted gluten-free bread or gluten-free crackers.

2 lbs pumpkin, peeled and cut into 1 inch cubes
1 Tbsp ghee
1 Tbsp olive oil
1 large onion, coarsely chopped
3 cups vegetable broth
1 bay leaf
1 cup canned, diced tomatoes, with their juice
¼ cup dry sherry or white wine

In a soup pot, heat the ghee and olive oil until the ghee is melted.
Sauté the onion and pumpkin cubes for about 5 minutes until onion is softened.
Add the broth and bay leaf and simmer for 15 minutes.
Add tomatoes and sherry or wine and continue cooking another 10-15 minutes, until pumpkin is tender.

Remove bay leaf.
Working in batches, transfer soup to blender and blend until smooth.
Add each batch back to soup pot and heat all to simmer.

Quinoa Millet Tabbouli

This tabbouli tastes so much like what we have eaten in Middle Eastern restaurants that you wouldn't know there was no bulgur wheat in it. Authentic Middle Eastern tabbouli is *mostly* parsley with very little grain; my version has a little more of the grain. **Kitchen tip:** parsley can be kept fresh by cutting off the last ½inch of the stems from a bunch of parsley and placing the bunch in a glass vase filled with cold water, like a "bouquet". Change the water daily. Serve the tabbouli as part of a Middle Eastern feast with hummus (see Snacks), Israeli chopped salad or Easy Greek Salad (page 77), and falafel.

2 cups cooked quinoa-millet*
Juice of 1 large lemon (about ¼ cup)
3 Tbsp olive oil
2 tsp dried mint (you can use more)
Dash sea salt
1 plum tomato, finely diced
1/3 large cucumber, peeled and finely diced
1 whole bunch of curly parsley (not Italian flat type), finely chopped, about 1½ cups
1 scallion, finely chopped

In a large serving bowl place chopped parsley, plum tomato, cucumber, scallion, and dried mint, and toss until combined.
In a small bowl or large measuring cup combine the olive oil, dash of salt, and lemon juice. Stir with a small whisk.
Add 2 cups of the cooled quinoa-millet to the parsley mixture. Pour the dressing over the tabbouli and toss with a fork to combine.
Tabbouli tastes best at room temperature. If you are not serving this right away, make sure you take it out of the refrigerator and bring to room temperature before serving.

Fluffy Quinoa-Millet

In a large skillet dry toast ½ cup whole quinoa and ½ cup whole millet over medium heat until fragrant and the grains are beginning to pop (you can hear this).

While the grains are toasting, boil 2 cups of water in a saucepan.

Add the toasted grains to the boiling water, turn down the heat to low, cover and cook about 15-20 minutes until the liquid is absorbed. Remove cover and fluff the grains with a fork. Put cover back on for 15 minutes. Fluff with fork.

Cool before using for the tabbouli.

You will have about 1 cup left over grain which you can use for breakfast or even sprinkle on your lunch salad. Or you can make extra quinoa-millet and simultaneously make the Black Bean-Corn-Quinoa salad.

Raw Rutabaga Salad

My husband's family introduced me to shredded roots like rutabaga and celeriac. Related to the turnip, rutabaga is actually very sweet for a vegetable and this salad brings out that natural sweetness. Rutabaga is also wonderful cubed and roasted with other root vegetables like carrot, sweet potato, and parsnip. This recipe is very simple to make and I hope you'll try rutabaga, especially if you've never eaten it raw.

$\frac{3}{4}$ lb rutabaga, peeled and shredded (about 4-5 cups)
$\frac{1}{2}$ cup paper thin slices of red onion
$\frac{1}{2}$ cup chopped parsley
$\frac{1}{2}$ tsp lemon zest
2 Tbsp fresh lemon juice
2 Tbsp olive oil
Salt and pepper to taste

Remove the waxy outer layer of the rutabaga and shred with a box grater or the shredder attachment of a food processor. Place the rutabaga in a serving bowl.

Add onion, parsley, and lemon zest and toss with a fork to combine.

Combine lemon juice and olive oil in a small bowl and sprinkle this over the salad. Toss with a fork to combine. Taste and season to your liking with salt and pepper.

Raw Shredded Beet Salad

Most beet recipes use cooked beets. Raw shredded beet has a milder flavor than cooked, and is delicious and colorful added to lettuce salads. This beet salad is slightly sweet, slightly spicy, and will make a beet lover out of any skeptic.

2½ cups shredded raw beets
¼ cup currants
3 Tbsp olive oil
2 Tbsp fresh lemon juice
2 tsp agave nectar
1 tsp ground allspice

Place the shredded beets and currants in a colorful bowl and toss with a fork to thoroughly combine.
Combine the olive oil, lemon juice, agave nectar, and allspice in a small bowl and stir with a small wire whisk.
Pour the dressing over the beets and toss with a fork.

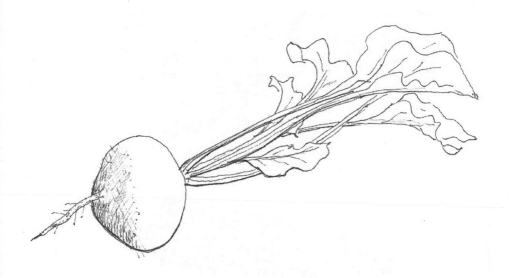

Roasted Beet Salad
Serves 4

Although I used to really dislike them, I've been growing beets in my garden for the last few years and have come to really enjoy them. Beets contain a fair amount of potassium and the beet greens are high in iron (3.3 mg per $\frac{1}{2}$ c cooked) and vitamin A (6100 iu/$\frac{1}{2}$ cup cooked). Greens can be sautéed in olive oil or ghee with some garlic and served as a side dish.

3-4 medium sized fresh beets
$\frac{1}{2}$ red onion, chopped or thinly sliced
3 Tbsp red wine vinegar
1 Tbsp extra virgin olive oil
$1\frac{1}{2}$ tsp Dijon mustard
Salt, pepper to taste
$\frac{1}{4}$ tsp tarragon, crushed

Wash beets and trim the leaves and root but do not peel.
Wrap beets in foil, making a package.
Place package in 400° oven and roast until tender, about an hour. You should be able to insert a fork easily.
Allow beets to cool before handling. Peel beets and cut into desired shape; cube, slice, or julienne.
Place beets in serving bowl and add onions.
Combine vinegar, olive oil, mustard, salt, pepper, and tarragon in measuring cup or small bowl and pour over beets.
Toss to combine.
Best if marinated for a couple of hours before eating or you can eat it right away.

Seaweed Slaw

This salad incorporates arame which is a type of sea vegetable. Arame is one of the milder tasting of the sea vegetables and it is quick and easy to prepare. Arame is great in salads like this slaw, or sautéed with julienne strips of firm vegetables like carrots and snow peas. Sea vegetables offer many nutrients such as calcium, magnesium, vitamin A, and of course iodine.

$\frac{1}{2}$ cup arame sea vegetable
$\frac{1}{2}$ lb green cabbage
$\frac{1}{2}$ green pepper (medium or large)
$\frac{1}{2}$ medium red onion
1 Tbsp wheat-free tamari
1 Tbsp mirin (rice wine)
1 Tbsp rice vinegar
2 tsp canola oil
2 tsp toasted sesame oil
2 tsp lime juice
$\frac{1}{2}$ cup cilantro, finely minced
1 Tbsp black sesame seeds

Rinse the arame in a colander under cold water.
Place the arame in a bowl and cover with water, 2 inches above the seaweed.
Let stand for 10 minutes. Drain* and place seaweed in a serving bowl.
Thinly slice the cabbage into long ribbons no wider than $\frac{1}{4}$ inch. Add to serving bowl.
Thinly slice the green pepper and add to serving bowl.
Slice the onion lengthwise into very thin strips. Add to serving bowl.

In a small bowl mix the tamari, mirin, rice vinegar, canola oil, sesame oil, and lime juice. Add this dressing to the seaweed and cabbage and toss with a fork to combine.
Add cilantro and toss again.
Sprinkle slaw with sesame seeds and serve.

*Save the seaweed soaking water to use for watering your plants. It has natural minerals that are great fertilizers for plants.

Zucchini Soup
4-5 servings

In their gardening days, my parents made this soup to take care of the zucchini overrun, but since it is very low in calories, easy to make, and delicious, they have been making it ever since. The original recipe started with chicken bouillon which is neither vegetarian nor gluten-free. If you use the ghee the soup will have a rich, buttery flavor. Though there is no cream, the soup is very creamy after it is puréed.

1 large onion, chopped
2 tablespoons ghee or olive oil
2 cups vegetable broth
4 cups diced zucchini
½ teaspoon salt
1/8 teaspoon each garlic powder and celery salt or seed
Dash pepper
¼ cup parsley leaves (less is ok)

In saucepan sauté onion in ghee or olive oil until tender.
Add remaining ingredients except parsley.
Cook over medium heat about 5 minutes or until zucchini is tender.
Carefully pour into blender (small amount at a time), add parsley and whirl at high speed until smooth.

If desired, thin soup with additional vegetable broth.
Serve hot or cold.

Summer Gazpacho
Makes about 8 cups

This is best when made in the summer at the height of tomato, cucumber, and basil harvest. The fresh basil adds a wonderful flavor and is very important to the recipe. The gazpacho is fast to prepare, worthy of company, and very refreshing for the hottest of evenings. The original recipe calls for the tomatoes to be peeled but I honestly cannot be bothered and the skins get pulverized and do not detract from the soup.

4 medium to large ripe tomatoes
2 cloves garlic
1 small onion
1 carrot, peeled
1 cucumber, peeled, and seeds removed
1 green pepper
¼ cup fresh parsley
¼ cup fresh basil leaves (or more!)
2-4 Tbsp olive oil (it is almost fat free if you use the smaller amount of oil)
¼ cup fresh lemon juice
3 cups tomato juice (preferably organic)

Cut the tomatoes into quarters or eights and pulse in a food processor until chopped into small dice.
Remove these to a large serving bowl.
Place the garlic, onion, carrot, cucumber, green pepper, parsley, and basil in the food processor and pulse several times until the vegetables are small dice and the herbs are tiny.
Add this to the tomatoes.
Stir in the tomato juice, olive oil, and lemon juice.
Stir to combine.
Serve in attractive colorful bowls.

Garnish with any or none of the following:
> raw sunflower seeds, alfalfa sprouts, cubed tofu, grated carrot, a sprinkle of fresh basil sliced into fine ribbons.

Dressings and Sauces

Balsamic Vinaigrette

1 shallot or garlic clove
$\frac{1}{4}$ cup balsamic vinegar
$\frac{1}{2}$ cup extra virgin olive oil
1 Tbsp maple syrup
1 Tbsp Dijon mustard
$\frac{1}{4}$ cup chopped fresh basil
Sea salt and pepper to taste

Combine all ingredients in the blender and puree. Thin with up to 4 Tbsp water if needed.

Blueberry Dressing
Delicious on spinach salad or any light lunch salad.

1 shallot
1 cup fresh blueberries
1 tsp salt
3 Tbsp pure maple syrup or agave nectar
$\frac{1}{2}$ cup raspberry vinegar
1 cup canola oil

Combine all ingredients in blender and blend until mixed.

Carrot Ginger Miso Dressing
Makes $\frac{3}{4}$ cup

Miso is a fermented soy food made by cooking soybeans, then mixing them with Koji, a grain that is inoculated with aspergillus spore, a type of fungus, and aging the mixture for about two years. Miso comes in many flavors but only the ones made from inoculated gluten-free grains like rice are gluten-free; some are derived from oat or barley. According to Great Eastern Sun, located in Asheville, North Carolina, the following types of miso produced by the company (using rice Koji) under the brand Miso Master are gluten-free: Organic Mellow White Miso, Organic Brown Rice Miso, Organic Sweet White Miso, Organic Traditional Red Miso, and Organic Chickpea Miso. I discuss the health benefits of miso in the section Good Nutrition Tips for Vegetarians.

If you love the dressing used in the Japanese restaurants as I do and always wondered how to make it, you'll be very happy to have this recipe.

1/3 cup shredded carrot
1 Tbsp fresh ginger, peeled and coarsely chopped
1 Tbsp Mellow White miso
5 Tbsp rice vinegar
5 Tbsp canola oil (for a lower fat version use only 1 Tbsp)
1 tsp wheat-free tamari
$\frac{1}{2}$ tsp pure maple syrup
$\frac{1}{4}$ tsp sea salt

Place all ingredients in the bowl of a food processor fitted with a steel blade.
Process until smooth.

YUM!

Josh's Guacamole

I named this mashed avocado spread after my son, who has
become the expert guacamole maker in our house.

1 fresh avocado
Juice of ½ lemon
1 garlic clove, crushed
Sea salt to taste

Cut avocado in half and remove the pit.
Scoop out avocado "flesh" into small bowl and mash with fork.
Crush garlic clove and add to avocado.
Add lemon juice and a sprinkle of salt to avocado.
Mash all together with a fork.

Maple Mustard Vinaigrette

Use the vinaigrette to marinate Portobello mushrooms before
grilling or use as a basting sauce for grilled vegetables.

½ cup canola oil
¼ cup maple syrup
¼ cup apple cider vinegar
2 Tbsp Dijon mustard
2 Tbsp wheat-free soy sauce
½ tsp salt
Freshly ground pepper

Place all ingredients in a bowl and combine using a wire whisk.

Pesto Sauces

Pesto sauce can be made in many varieties to add intense flavor to whatever you are cooking; it pumps up the taste of foods that are missing the cheese topping. I have found basil pesto to freeze very well, although cilantro pesto will not hold up in the freezer. These pesto sauces without cheese can be used on gluten-free pasta, in soups, as a spread to add flavor to sandwiches, as a base instead of tomato sauce for gluten-free pizza. Try my *Black Bean Tortilla Pizza* (see Main Dishes) which uses cilantro pesto. Be creative and invent your own!

Fresh Basil Pesto
$\frac{1}{2}$ lb fresh basil, woody stems removed
$\frac{1}{2}$ cup pine nuts
$\frac{1}{2}$ cup olive oil
4 large garlic cloves
$\frac{1}{2}$ tsp sea salt

Combine all ingredients in food processor and puree until a smooth paste is formed

Cilantro Pesto
2 garlic cloves
1 bunch fresh cilantro, washed well, stems trimmed
$\frac{1}{4}$ cup olive oil
1/3 cup raw pine nuts
Pinch sea salt

Place all ingredients in food processor. Process with steel blade until well-pulverized and somewhat spreadable. Use the pesto for any dish that has a Mexican flavor.

Sundried Tomato Pesto
$\frac{3}{4}$ cup dried tomatoes soaked in very hot water to cover for 10 minutes and then drained
$\frac{3}{4}$ cup pitted black olives (optional, but great with them)
2 large cloves garlic
1 cup chopped fresh parsley or basil
$\frac{1}{2}$ cup pine nuts
$\frac{1}{2}$ cup olive oil

Blend in blender or food processor until smooth.

Raspberry Vinaigrette

$\frac{1}{4}$ cup raspberry vinegar
$\frac{1}{4}$ cup olive oil
1 tsp Dijon mustard
1 shallot
1 Tbsp maple syrup

Combine all ingredients in blender and blend until mixed.

Sandwich and Wrap Spreads
A few ideas for wraps and sandwiches

Chipotle Dressing
Mix 1 tsp sauce from a can of chipotle chilies (they have a wonderfully smoky flavor) with $\frac{1}{2}$ cup of plain soy yogurt. Serve this as a sauce for a wrap of black beans, rice, roasted vegetables, shredded lettuce, and avocado or guacamole.

Basil Pesto Mayo
Mix 1 Tbsp prepared dairy-free basil pesto with 2-4 Tbsp vegan mayo. Use as a spread for sandwiches or roasted Portobello mushroom sandwiches.

Sesame Garlic Dressing
Makes 1¼ cups

I first had this dressing about 25 years ago at a vegetarian restaurant in the Village in NYC called Whole Wheat and Wild Berries. I liked it so much that I asked for the recipe. The original recipe called for a cup of oil which I've replaced with part oil and part water. This reduces the fat considerably. If you prefer more oil you can use 1 cup of oil and no water, or whatever proportions of oil and water that you like.

1 inch piece of fresh ginger, peeled
3 cloves garlic
½ cup canola oil
Juice of 1 lemon
2 Tbsp wheat-free tamari
2 Tbsp sesame tahini
½ cup water

Place all ingredients in a food processor fitted with steel blade. Blend until smooth.

Tofu Sour Cream

1 box silken tofu (12 oz Mori-Nu vacuum packed)
2 Tbsp cider vinegar
1 Tbsp canola oil
¼ tsp sea salt

Place all ingredients in blender and blend until smooth.

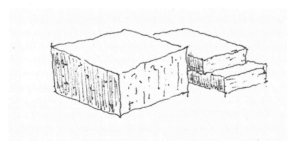

Main Dish Salads, Soups and Stews

Zelda's Tempeh Stew
Serves 4

Our dear friend Zelda went on a Macrobiotic diet after her diagnosis with breast cancer. This was one of the special dishes she would make. She took the time to cut the carrots into flower shapes which made it even more special. Serve tempeh and sauce over a bed of soba noodles with a side of broccoli and carrots.

8 ounces tempeh (wild rice, vegetable, flax, or soy)
2 Tbsp toasted sesame oil
1 Tbsp white miso (rice based)
1 Tbsp prepared mustard, Dijon works well
$\frac{1}{4}$ cup sauerkraut, preferably organic
1-2 cups water
2 Tbsp arrowroot powder dissolved in $\frac{1}{4}$ cup water*
1 bunch broccoli florets
$\frac{1}{2}$ pound carrots, thinly sliced on the diagonal
100% buckwheat soba noodles (some soba noodles contain wheat flour as well as buckwheat flour, make sure the noodles are 100% buckwheat)

Cut tempeh into 1-inch cubes.
Heat oil in skillet and pan-fry until golden.
Combine miso, mustard, sauerkraut, water, and arrowroot mixture to make sauce. Add sauce to tempeh in skillet and simmer until bubbling. Simmer 15 minutes.
Lightly steam carrots and broccoli together until tender but retaining their color and not mushy.
Cook soba noodles according to package directions.

*you may substitute tapioca starch for the arrowroot

Buckwheat and Bean Chili
Makes about 8 cups

This looks like it has a long list of ingredients but it really goes together quickly. This chili offers Vitamin A from the carrots and sweet potato, vitamin C from the peppers, lycopene from the tomatoes, protein and fiber from the pinto beans and buckwheat. It is very thick and can also be used as the base for a tamale pie with a cornbread-like topping, see recipe below.

1 Tbsp canola oil
1 large onion, roughly chopped
2 cloves garlic, chopped
1 large green pepper, coarsely chopped
2 carrots, peeled and diced
1 Tbsp chili powder
2 tsp ground cumin
2 tsp oregano
$\frac{1}{2}$ tsp ground coriander
2 Tbsp tomato paste
$1\frac{1}{4}$ cup water
1 (14-16 oz) can diced tomatoes, **_undrained_**
$\frac{1}{2}$ cup whole buckwheat groats (kasha)
1 Tbsp gluten-free brown rice syrup (or maple syrup)
1 (14-16oz) can pinto beans, rinsed and drained (black beans are also good!)
$\frac{1}{2}$ cup frozen corn
1 cooked sweet potato, peeled and cubed (about 1 cup cubes)
$\frac{1}{2}$ cup chopped cilantro
Sea salt to taste
Chopped avocado for garnish

Chop all the vegetables and place in bowls, keeping the onion and garlic together in one bowl and the carrots and green pepper together in another bowl.
In a medium sized soup pot heat the oil and cook the onion and garlic over medium heat for about 2 minutes.

Add the green pepper and carrots and cook for another two minutes.

Add the chili powder, cumin, oregano, and coriander and cook for about 30 seconds, stirring.

Add the tomato paste, water, diced tomatoes with their juice, buckwheat groats, and brown rice syrup.

Cover the pan and cook for 15 minutes, periodically stirring the chili to make sure it does not stick to the bottom.

After 15 minutes, remove the cover, add the beans and corn and stir to combine.

Add the sweet potato and cilantro and stir to combine.

Salt to taste.

Serve the chili in bowls with chopped avocado on top.

Tamale Pie

To make the chili into a tamale pie, pour the chili into an oven-safe casserole. Combine the ingredients below and spread this over the chili. Bake the tamale pie at 400° for 15-20 minutes until the cornbread topping is set and slightly brown.

1 cup corn meal
1 $\frac{1}{2}$ tsp baking powder
$\frac{1}{4}$ tsp salt
1 egg
$\frac{1}{2}$ cup plain soy milk
2 Tbsp canola oil

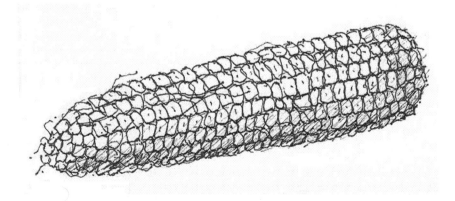

Cuban Black Beans
About 8 servings

This recipe came by way of a close friend whose roommate grew up in Florida enjoying this family recipe for black beans. The original recipe calls for ½ cup olive oil which tastes wonderful but is too much fat, even if it is a "good fat", for my needs. I've reduced the oil to ¼ cup and you can reduce it further to 2 tablespoons if you want even less fat. You can also try the recipe with the full amount of oil. Use a high quality olive oil, preferably extra virgin, which imparts a strong fruity olive flavor. The kombu seaweed which I add during the cooking of the beans helps to tenderize them, and contributes alkalizing properties to the broth. Serve the beans with rice and some chopped avocado. The beans freeze very well so if you find this recipe makes too much, freeze some in 2 cup containers for another day.

1 lb black beans
A 2-3 inch piece of kombu seaweed
1 medium onion, chopped
½ green pepper, chopped
2 cloves garlic, minced
1 tsp crushed oregano
1 bay leaf
2 Tbsp red wine vinegar
2-4 Tbsp good quality olive oil
Sea salt and pepper to taste

Wash the beans in a colander and discard the imperfect ones. In a 3-4 quart soup pot, place the beans, kombu, and water to cover about 2-3 inches above the beans.
Bring to a boil then reduce heat to simmer. Cook until the beans are tender, 45-60 minutes. When fully cooked, remove what is left of the kombu.
Add the rest of the ingredients and continue cooking until the beans thicken.

Leftover beans can be made into refried beans. In a large skillet heat 1-2 Tbsp oil over medium heat and sauté ½ of a chopped onion and 2 cloves minced garlic. If you have a jalapeno chili, add about 1-2 tsp minced (or more if you like it really hot). Add the leftover black beans and mash them with a potato masher as they cook with the oil and onions. They are ready when they are mashed to your liking, and heated all the way through.

Serve refried beans in a tortilla with chopped red onion, avocado, salsa, and anything else you have in your refrigerator that goes.

Dilly of a Rice Salad
Serves 4 as a main dish

When I became vegetarian my dad would always look for recipes that would meet my needs and taste good as well. This is a simple recipe that works as a summer main dish salad or something to bring to a barbecue.

3 cups cooked rice (white or brown, long grain or short)
1 can (15 oz.) red kidney beans, rinsed and drained
1 medium carrot, chopped
½ cup sliced celery
¼ cup thinly sliced green onions
¼ cup cider vinegar
¼ cup canola oil
1 tablespoon maple syrup
½ teaspoon powdered mustard
½ teaspoon dill weed*
¼ teaspoon sea salt

Combine all but liquid. Then combine liquid and toss with rice.
*This is especially good when fresh dill is in season. If using fresh dill, use a couple tablespoons or to taste.

Kale Salad

Serves 4 as a main dish salad

Kale is a leafy green vegetable that provides calcium, Vitamin K, Vitamin C, iron, and lots of Vitamin A. It is full of antioxidants! Though kale is usually seen in recipes as a cooked vegetable, this salad uses raw kale. It was inspired by a salad I enjoy often at the Whole Earth Center in Princeton, New Jersey. The whole recipe has approximately 1600 calories. Enjoy!

4 oz. fresh kale, raw, cut or torn into 2-inch pieces
1½ cups cooked short grain brown rice
2 Tbsp raw sesame seeds
2 cups thinly sliced red cabbage
1 carrot, shredded
½ cup whole almonds, lightly toasted
½ lb firm tofu, drained and pressed* and cut into cubes

Dressing:
6 Tbsp canola oil
6 Tbsp fresh lemon juice
1 Tbsp wheat-free tamari or soy sauce
1 tsp sesame oil

Combine salad ingredients in a large bowl and toss until combined.
Combine dressing ingredients in a small bowl and add to salad.
Toss until the kale leaves are coated with dressing.
Best if allowed to rest for an hour or so before serving so that the kale leaves have a chance to wilt slightly.

* to press tofu:
Wrap the tofu cake in a clean absorbent kitchen towel (I find a real towel works better than a paper towel) and place the wrapped tofu on a plate. Place a cutting board on the plate and top that with a very heavy object.
I use a cast iron pan or a tea kettle filled with water.

Allow the tofu to drain into the towel for about 30 minutes. Remove the towel and slice or cube the tofu.

Black Bean, Corn, & Quinoa Salad
Serves 4 as a main dish

I used to make this with barley in our pre-gluten-free days. It was the salad that I brought to swim team banquets and other pot luck suppers and I always came home with an empty bowl. It goes together quickly, can be made any time of the year, and got rave reviews by my testers.

2 cans black beans, rinsed and drained
1 cup chopped fresh cilantro
1 red pepper, diced
$\frac{1}{2}$ -1 cup diced red onion
2 cups frozen corn kernels (steamed until tender, 2-3 minutes)
1$\frac{1}{2}$ cups cooked and cooled quinoa* ($\frac{3}{4}$ cup quinoa to 1$\frac{1}{2}$ cups water)

Dressing:
Juice of 2 limes or 1 large lemon
1 clove garlic, minced
2 Tbsp canola oil
$\frac{1}{4}$ tsp ground cumin
Salt to taste
Combine salad ingredients in a large bowl. Combine dressing ingredients in a small bowl and stir gently into salad, tossing until fully combined.

* Cooking quinoa
Use 1 part quinoa to 2 parts water
        (1 cup quinoa to 2 cups water)
Place 1 cup dry quinoa in a dry skillet over medium-low heat and cook gently, stirring frequently so that it does not burn. Meanwhile, bring 2 cups water to a boil in a separate pot. When the quinoa begins to pop, add it to the boiling water and simmer over medium heat until water is fully absorbed (about 18 minutes). Fluff with a fork.

Lemony Chickpea & Rice Salad
Serves 4 for dinner

This salad is very lemony with both fresh lemon juice and lemon peel of a whole lemon. **Kitchen tip**: keep the peels from lemons that have been juiced in an easy-to-retrieve bag in the refrigerator. If you will not be using grated lemon zest within a week of storing the lemon peels, grate the zest onto a piece of waxed paper and transfer the zest to a small freezer-safe bag. Freeze until needed for recipes. I would not use the frozen zest for fresh dishes like salads, however, it will work just fine in baked goods like muffins and waffles. Serve as a main dish with soup or vegetable salad. Or bring as picnic fare with an array of other alfresco items.

3 cups cooked basmati rice (white or brown)
$\frac{1}{4}$ cup sun-dried tomatoes (not oil packed), soaked for 10 minutes in **very** hot water, drained and then chopped
3 scallions, thinly sliced
Grated peel of 1 lemon
1 can chickpeas, rinsed and drained
1 14-oz can artichoke hearts (not in oil), drained and cut into chunks

$\frac{1}{4}$ cup vegetable broth
2 Tbsp extra virgin olive oil
2 Tbsp fresh lemon juice
2 garlic cloves, minced
1 tsp Dijon mustard
$\frac{1}{2}$ tsp oregano
Sea salt
Freshly ground black pepper to taste

In a large bowl combine rice, chopped sun-dried tomatoes, scallions, lemon peel, chickpeas, and artichoke hearts.
In a large glass measuring cup combine vegetable broth, olive oil, lemon juice, garlic cloves, mustard, oregano, salt and pepper. Stir to combine. Add dressing to salad and toss to combine.

Creamy Mushroom Brown Rice Soup

This soup used to be a creamy mushroom-barley soup made with milk. One of my testers is not a mushroom lover and really liked the soup. Another of my testers thought the brown rice was barley (or expected it to be). Substitute canola oil for the ghee to make this vegan.

1 tsp ghee
½ cup chopped onion
8 oz fresh mushrooms, sliced
4 cups vegetable broth
½ cup brown rice (preferably short grain)
¼ of an 8-inch square of Nori sea vegetable
¼ tsp umeboshi plum paste
½ tsp white (rice) miso
Couple drops hot pepper sauce
3 Tbsp potato starch
½ cup unsweetened soy milk
1 cup unsweetened soy milk
3 Tbsp dry sherry
Freshly ground black pepper
Sea salt
2 Tbsp chopped fresh parsley

In a 4 quart saucepan melt ghee. Add onion and mushrooms and sauté until softened. Add 3 cups of the broth, the brown rice, Nori, plum paste, miso, and hot pepper sauce, and bring to a boil. Lower heat to a simmer and cook covered about 30 minutes until rice is tender.
Measure the potato starch into a small bowl and add ½ cup soy milk, whisking until smooth. Add this into the soup.
Add remaining 1 cup of soy milk. Add 4th cup broth.
Add sherry. Add salt and pepper to taste.
Right before serving, stir in fresh parsley.

Lentils Mexicanos
Makes 4-6 servings

My mom started making this after I came home from college and announced that I was vegetarian and it was always one of my favorites. The original recipe had Monterey jack cheese melted on the top but other than that I didn't have to change much. It is good without any cheese, or you can use vegan cheese if you like. In our house a separate bowl of shredded cheese is put on the table for the cheese eaters. If you are using the vegan cheese, sprinkle the cheese onto the lentils before baking. After baking for 15 minutes, place baking dish under broiler for a few minutes until vegan cheese is bubbly.

1 cup lentils, rinsed and drained
2 cups water
1 cup chopped onion
1 clove garlic, chopped finely
1 Tbsp vegetable oil
½ cup sliced black olives
1 can (28 ounces) diced tomatoes, or 2 16 oz. cans
1 7-ounce can diced green chilies
1 teaspoon ground cumin
½ tsp sea salt
½ cup chopped cilantro
2 cups plain gluten-free tortilla chips (or you can make rice)
Monterey Jack flavored casein-free cheese (Follow Your Heart), 1 cup shredded (optional)

Simmer lentils in water, covered, until just tender, about 30 minutes. Sauté onion and garlic in oil until translucent.
Add tomatoes, chilies, cumin, and salt to onion mix and cook until heated through. Combine with lentils.
Stir in cilantro and olives.
Spread mixture in 9 x 9inch baking dish.
Bake 350° F about 15 minutes.
Serve in bowls with chips to scoop up the lentils or with large tostada chips or corn tortillas.
Top with chopped avocado or guacamole.

Spinach Lentil Salad
Serves 4

Black Beluga lentils are very small, black and shiny and make a rather elegant salad. If you can't find black lentils, small green French lentils would work just as well. The ingredients in this recipe are readily available all year so it is easily made, winter or summer. Serve it on pretty salad plates with a sliced pear or orange, and a light vegetable soup.

3/4 cup Black Beluga lentils
$\frac{1}{2}$ cup chopped scallions
1/3 cup chopped Kalamata olives
$\frac{1}{2}$ cup sun dried tomatoes, soaked in hot water for 10 minutes and chopped
$\frac{1}{2}$ cup fresh parsley, minced
$\frac{1}{4}$ cup fresh basil, finely chopped
Grated zest of $\frac{1}{2}$ lemon
1 bag of baby spinach (8-10 oz)

Dressing
1 Tbsp fresh lemon juice
1 clove garlic, minced
1 tsp Dijon mustard
2 Tbsp extra virgin olive oil
Sea salt and pepper to taste

Cook the lentils in $1\frac{1}{2}$ cups water about 30 minutes until tender and the water has been absorbed. Allow the lentils to cool. Drain if there is still water in the pan and transfer to a large bowl.
Add to the lentils the scallions, olives, sun dried tomatoes, parsley, basil, and lemon zest. Lightly stir with a fork to combine.
Mix the dressing and pour it over the lentil mixture.
Add the spinach to the lentils and combine by folding the spinach into the salad so that the dressing and lentils are evenly distributed.

Mulligatawny
Serves 4 generously

An Indian-spiced soup with plenty of protein from the chickpeas, it works well for a meal along with some type of raw salad.

1 teaspoon olive oil
½ cup chopped onions
1 stalk celery, diced
1 apple, peeled and diced
3-5 cloves of garlic, minced
1 carrot diced
3 tablespoons potato starch flour
3 teaspoons curry (may be reduced to taste)
¼ teaspoon each ginger, cinnamon, turmeric, and 1/8 tsp cayenne (Omit the cayenne if you don't like hot)
5 cups vegetable broth
1 14 oz can chickpeas, rinsed and drained
1 16 oz. can diced tomatoes
1 bay leaf
1 tablespoon lemon juice
½ cup coconut milk
½ cup chopped cilantro

Sauté onions in olive oil over medium heat until they are transparent and soft, not browned.
Keep the heat at medium and add the celery, apple, garlic, and carrot and cook about 4-5 minutes until the vegetables are softened.
Add the potato starch flour, curry, ginger, cinnamon, turmeric, and cayenne if using, and cook 2 minutes until vegetables are coated with the flour. The mixture will be a thick mush.
Stir in vegetable broth, chickpeas, tomatoes, and bay leaf.
Bring to a boil, cover, and simmer 20 minutes.
Remove bay leaf and add lemon juice.
Allow to cool.

Put in a blender (or food processor) and puree.

Return soup to pot and reheat over medium heat.
Turn flame down to simmer and add the coconut milk.
Heat gently; do not boil.
Add cilantro right before serving.

Summer Pasta Salad
Serves 4 as a main dish

A creamy pasta salad with lots of fresh dill and edamame for protein, it is simple to make and easy to take to an outdoor event.

½lb gluten-free brown rice pasta penne or small shells
1 Tbsp olive oil
1 green pepper, cut into 1 inch squares
½ cup diced red onion
1 cup halved grape tomatoes
½ cup diced sweet pickles
½ cup sliced scallions
½ cup frozen edamame, steamed 1-2 minutes, then cooled
¾ cup shredded peeled carrot
½ cup sliced celery
¼ cup finely chopped fresh dill
½ cup tofu sour cream (see Dressings and Sauces)
¼ cup vegan mayonnaise
2 tsp red wine vinegar
Pinch sea salt

Cook brown rice pasta according to package instructions, drain, and place in a large bowl with 1 Tbsp olive oil.
Add to the pasta the green pepper, red onion, grape tomatoes, sweet pickles, scallions, edamame, shredded carrot, celery, and dill.
Fold vegetables into pasta until evenly distributed.
Combine tofu sour cream, vegan mayonnaise, and red wine vinegar.
Add tofu mixture to the pasta and vegetables and fold to combine. Add salt to taste

.Quinoa "Cous Cous"

My mother made a couscous salad long before it became mainstream. Of course the original was made with couscous, a version of semolina wheat, which is not gluten-free. I have substituted a quinoa-millet mix with excellent results.

2 cups water or gluten-free vegetable broth
1 Tbsp olive oil
1/8 tsp turmeric
1/8 tsp ground cinnamon
1/8 tsp ground ginger
$\frac{1}{2}$ cup quinoa
$\frac{1}{2}$ cup millet
$\frac{1}{4}$ cup raisins
$\frac{1}{4}$ cup chopped dates (make sure they are whole, pitted dates, not floured)
$\frac{1}{2}$ cup shredded carrots
1 cup shredded zucchini
$\frac{1}{4}$ cup chopped onion
1 medium tomato, chopped
1 cup chickpeas, drained, and rinsed

Dressing
1 tbsp olive oil
1 $\frac{1}{2}$ Tbsp lemon juice

Finish
$\frac{1}{4}$ cup slivered almonds, lightly toasted

Toast the millet and quinoa in a dry skillet over medium heat until fragrant.
Meanwhile, bring the water or broth to a boil with 1 Tbsp olive oil, the turmeric, cinnamon, and ginger.
Add the toasted millet-quinoa to the boiling broth, turn down heat to simmer, cover, and cook about 15-20 minutes until the liquid is fully absorbed.
Remove cover and fluff with a fork.
Add raisins and dates, and cover until fully cooled.

Fluff again with a fork.

Place cooled millet-quinoa in a large serving bowl.

Add shredded carrots, shredded zucchini, chopped onion, tomato, and chickpeas.

Toss to combine.

Combine dressing ingredients in small bowl and drizzle over the couscous.

Sprinkle with toasted almonds right before serving

Hearty Soup Mix

This is easy to mix together and keep in a jar. To make the soup, just put 1 cup soup mix and four cups water or vegetable broth in a large soup pan. Add 2 chopped, carrots, 1 chopped onion, 1-2 stalks celery chopped, 1 16 oz can diced tomatoes, 2-4 Tbsp tomato paste, and 1 bay leaf. You may also add any other herbs that you like such as parsley or cilantro or basil. Additional vegetables that work well: 1 parsnip chopped, 1 cup chopped rutabaga, diced turnip, chopped sweet or white potato. Once made, the soup freezes well.

1 cup green split peas
1 cup yellow split peas
1 cup red lentils
1 cup brown lentils
1 cup gluten-free alphabet pasta (I use Mrs. Leeper's)
1 cup brown rice (preferably short grain)

South of the Border Soup with Tortilla Confetti
Serves 4 as a main dish with leftovers

This packs enough protein to use for a main dish soup. If you are very gluten-sensitive, please be sure to use gluten-free corn tortillas (Food For Life is one brand). Serve with a green salad and sliced avocado. Serve fresh orange slices on the salad or separately for some extra color.

1 Tbsp vegetable oil
3 cloves garlic, minced
1 small onion, chopped
¾ tsp ground cumin
½ tsp chili powder
1 14-16 oz can of diced tomatoes
1 pound firm or extra-firm tofu cut into cubes
4 cups fresh or frozen corn, or 2 cans hominy, drained
1 (15-ounce) can black beans, rinsed and drained
1 4.5-7-oz can diced mild green chilies
Jalapeno pepper, minced (optional)
1 cup shredded carrot (1-2 medium)
2 cups vegetable broth
¼ cup chopped cilantro (may be doubled)
Juice of half a fresh lime (about 1 Tbsp)
Salt and pepper, to taste

Heat oil over medium-high heat in a large saucepan or Dutch oven.
Add garlic and onion and cook until tender but not browned.
Add cumin and chili powder and cook for several seconds.
Add tomatoes and cook for a few minutes more.
Add the tofu cubes and stir gently until heated through.
Add the corn, black beans, green chilies, jalapeno if using, carrot, vegetable broth, and cilantro.
Bring to gentle boil, then reduce heat and simmer for about 15 to 20 minutes to let flavors blend.
Season with salt and pepper to taste.
Stir in the lime juice before serving.
Garnish each bowl with tortilla confetti.

Tortilla Confetti
Stack 5 gluten-free corn tortillas and cut the stack in half.
Julienne strips of the tortillas until both stacks are used.
Heat 1 Tbsp oil in a skillet over medium heat.
Add tortilla confetti to skillet and cook over medium heat
stirring constantly until the confetti strips are crisp and
golden brown.

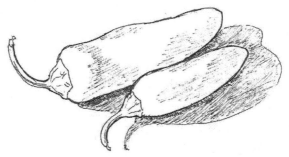

Rice Salad with Dates & Cashews
Serves 4 as a main dish

This is another salad that was inspired by something delicious
at the Whole Earth Center in Princeton, New Jersey. Though
there are few ingredients, this salad is addictive and we all
fight over the leftovers (if there are any!).

3 cups cooked brown rice (long or short grain)*
4-5 scallions, both green and white parts, sliced
$\frac{3}{4}$ cup cashews, lightly toasted
1-2 tsp dried dill
$\frac{1}{2}$ cup chopped dates (gluten-free, no flour-coated dates)
2 Tbsp fresh lemon juice
2 Tbsp canola oil

In a large bowl combine all ingredients, tossing lightly until
combined.
*$1\frac{1}{2}$ cups uncooked rice combined with 3 cups water should
yield 3 cups of cooked rice

Virginia's Favorite Vegetable Soup

I served a version of this soup to my friend Virginia and she liked it so much she wrote down the recipe. She then made it for her family who declared it was the best vegetable soup they had ever had. The parsnip and turnip add unique flavor to the soup and the lentils provide plenty of protein. Serve with a colorful salad and some gluten-free corn muffins.

6 cups gluten-free vegetable broth
1 medium onion, chopped
2 medium potatoes, cubed
2 carrots, diced
2 stalks celery, diced
1 medium parsnip, peeled and diced
1 medium turnip, peeled and diced
½ cup red lentils
½ cup brown lentils
3 cups tomato juice
1 clove garlic, minced
1 Tbsp tomato paste
1 (14-16oz) can diced tomatoes
1 bay leaf
1 Tbsp wheat-free soy sauce
¼ cup chopped parsley
2 Tbsp prepared basil pesto (see *Dressings and Sauces*)

Place vegetable broth in a large soup pot and begin heating over medium heat.
Add all vegetables, lentils, tomato juice, garlic, tomato paste, diced tomatoes, and bay leaf to broth. Bring to a simmer over medium heat.
Turn heat to low and continue cooking for about 1 hour or until vegetables and lentils are tender.
Add soy sauce, parsley, and pesto and cook for another 10 minutes over low heat until flavors are bended.

Raw Shredded Beet Salad

Black Bean Corn Quinoa Salad

Lemony Rice and Chickpea Salad

Spinach Lentil Salad

Broccoli Tomato Pasta

Tempeh Bacon BLT

Black Bean Tortilla Pizza

Easy Greek Salad

Rosemary Shortbread

Raw Carrot Cake

Banana Chocolate Chip Minis

Main Dishes

Black Bean Tortilla Pizza
Serves 4

I used to make these with flour tortillas but they are just as good with corn tortillas. These got rave reviews from my testers. For those who are very gluten-sensitive, make sure you get gluten-free corn tortillas.

1 recipe cilantro pesto (see *Dressings and Sauces*)
8 medium-sized gluten-free corn tortillas (I especially like the real Mexican corn tortillas which are a little thicker)
1 can black beans, rinsed and drained
1 red pepper, diced
3-4 plum tomatoes, diced
½ large red onion, diced
Vegan cheese, shredded (optional, Follow Your Heart Vegan Monterey Jack would be a good option)

Set oven to 350° and lay tortillas on racks in oven. Bake for about 5 minutes or until slightly hardened but not browned or crumbly.
Lay the tortillas on a baking sheet, slightly overlapping is ok. You can get 4-6 on a baking tray.
Spread cilantro pesto on tortillas, using all of the pesto, spreading it evenly amongst the tortillas.
Top each tortilla with ¼ cup black beans, 1 Tbsp red onion, 1 Tbsp red pepper, and 1 Tbsp chopped tomato.
Bake the pizzas for about 7 minutes until the vegetables are heated through.

If you like, you can use shredded vegan gluten-free casein-free cheese. Shred the cheese and sprinkle each pizza with about 2-4 Tbsp. After heating the pizzas for 7 min. put the tray under the broiler to melt the cheese; broil until the cheese is bubbly.

113

Artichoke Sundried Tomato Risotto
Serves 6 hearty appetites

I especially like to use a large Wok for cooking risotto because it gives me lots of room to stir the rice and add lots of vegetables. This recipe makes a lot. You will be surprised at how creamy risotto can be despite the lack of cheese. This recipe received excellent reviews from my testers who included some inexperienced risotto makers.

6 cups vegetable broth
2 Tbsp olive oil
4 garlic cloves, minced or pressed
1 cup chopped onion
1½ cups Arborio rice
¼ cup dry white wine
1 14-ounce can of artichoke hearts, drained and quartered
½ cup sundried tomatoes, soaked in hot water for 10 min. and chopped
¼ cup pitted Kalamata olives, chopped
¼ cup chopped fresh basil or 2-4 Tbsp dairy-free basil pesto
Grated rind of 1 lemon
¼ cup pine nuts, lightly toasted

In a saucepan, bring the broth to a boil and then reduce the heat to maintain a gentle simmer.
In a large, heavy saucepan or wok on medium-high heat, cook the onion in the olive oil 4-5 minutes until translucent.
Add the garlic and rice, stirring to coat each grain with oil.
Add 1 cup of broth and cook until most of the liquid is absorbed.
Stir the risotto between each addition of broth making sure to scrape the bottom of the saucepan or wok. A non-metal spatula allows you to get underneath the risotto with a kind of folding motion.
Add 2nd cup of broth and cook until most of the broth is absorbed.
Add 3rd cup of broth and cook until most of the liquid is absorbed.

Add the sundried tomatoes and the 4th cup of broth and continue cooking until the liquid is absorbed.

Add olives, artichokes, and wine along with the 5th cup of broth and cook until liquid is absorbed. The rice will be getting soft and creamy looking.

Add the 6th and final cup of broth and the basil or pesto and cook until the liquid is absorbed.

Add the lemon rind right before serving.

Garnish with toasted pine nuts.

Broccoli-Tomato Pasta
Serves at least 4 including a teenage boy
Cut the recipe in half for smaller portions and no leftovers.

1 lb gluten-free pasta, preferably small shells shape
3 large cloves garlic, minced
4 cups fresh broccoli florets (can be prepackaged to save time)
$1\frac{1}{2}$ cups chopped fresh plum tomatoes (even winter ones will be ok)
$\frac{1}{2}$ cup Kalamata olives, chopped
2 Tbsp olive oil
2 Tbsp pine nuts
Freshly ground pepper

Cook the pasta according to package directions. During the last three minutes of cooking the pasta, add the broccoli. Drain both and place in a large serving bowl.

Heat 1 Tbsp olive oil in a small sauté pan and warm the garlic over low heat until fragrant, about 20 seconds. Be careful not to burn garlic.

Add garlic to pasta, scraping the flavored oil from the sauté pan with a spatula.

Add tomatoes, olives, pine nuts, and 2nd Tbsp olive oil. Toss all together, add freshly ground pepper if desired, and serve immediately.

This is good hot, at room temperature, or cold for lunch the next day.

Beans and Greens
Serves 4 hungry people

A very simple but delicious combination of potato, kale, tomato, and white beans, with lots of garlic, this dish is quite filling without contributing tons of calories. Serve with a green salad or colorful carrot salad.

1 lb fresh kale, washed and leaves stripped from the stems
1 lb Yukon gold potatoes (about 4 fist-sized potatoes), scrubbed, skins on
3 large cloves garlic, minced
1/8 tsp red pepper flakes
1 Tbsp olive oil
1 16-oz can diced tomatoes
1 16-oz can small white beans, rinsed and drained
1 Tbsp fresh lemon juice
$\frac{1}{4}$ tsp sea salt
Freshly ground black pepper

Fill a small soup pan about $\frac{3}{4}$ with water and set over high flame to boil.
Rip the kale leaves from the center ribs and tear them into bite-size pieces. Place these in a bowl and set aside.
Cut the potatoes lengthwise in half then slice these into half-moons, about $\frac{1}{4}$-inch thick. Place potato slices in a separate bowl.
Mince garlic. Squeeze lemon juice. Drain and rinse the beans. Open the tomatoes.
When water boils, add potato slices and boil for about 5 minutes or until tender.
Add kale and cook another two minutes.
Scoop out 1 cup of the cooking broth and reserve in a small bowl before draining the kale and potatoes in a colander.
In a large skillet (cast iron works well) heat olive oil over medium heat.
Add garlic and red pepper flakes and sauté for about 30 seconds.
Add the potato-kale mixture and toss to combine.

116

Add the tomatoes, beans, ½ cup cooking broth, lemon juice, salt, and pepper and fold together to combine.
Taste for seasoning and add more salt and pepper if needed.
Sprinkle with nutritional yeast if desired.

Gallo Pinto
Serves 4 with maybe some left over for lunch

We ate Gallo Pinto every day in Costa Rica where it's served for breakfast. Here at home we enjoy it for dinner. In Costa Rica the vegetables were cut into the tiniest pieces so try to get your dice as fine as possible. It works best if you use cooked rice that has been refrigerated overnight.

4 cups cooked white rice (preferably organic)
3 cups cooked black beans (cooked from scratch or canned if rinsed and drained)
2 Bell peppers in two different colors (red & green, red & yellow, etc.), finely diced
1 medium onion, finely diced
1 Tbsp olive oil
1 cup minced cilantro
½ tsp ground cumin
¼ tsp cardamom
Salt to taste

Heat the oil in a large skillet.
Add the onion and peppers and cook over medium heat until very soft.
Add the ground cumin and ground cardamom and cook briefly until combined.
Add the rice and cook while folding in the cooked vegetables.
Add the beans and fold these in.
Turn off heat and fold in the cilantro.
Season to taste with salt.

Blackeye Peas and Rice Plus Greens

Serves 4 for dinner plus enough leftovers for lunches

Blackeye peas and rice, or Hoppin' John, is traditional Southern food, thought to bring a year full of luck when served on New Year's Day. It is usually made with bacon or ham hock, for which I have substituted some tempeh bacon. This dish is traditionally served with some collard greens, and either sweet potatoes or cornbread.

½ pound blackeye peas, soaked overnight in water to cover
1 Tbsp olive oil
½ large onion, chopped
2 garlic cloves, minced
1 stalk celery, finely chopped
3 pieces tempeh bacon, already cooked, crumbled
1 cup organic white rice
A few drops hot sauce
Salt and pepper to taste

Drain pre-soaked peas and add to large pot with water to cover by an inch.
Sauté onion, garlic and celery in 1 Tbsp olive oil until softened. Add to pot with beans and bring to boil.
Turn down to medium heat and cook until beans are tender.
Add rice, crumbled tempeh bacon, hot sauce, and 2 additional cups water.
Cook over medium heat until rice is cooked and water is absorbed. Stir frequently so it does not burn and stick to the bottom of the pot.
Season with salt and pepper.

<u>Sautéed Collard Greens</u>
2 bunches Collard greens, washed and stems removed
5-6 large cloves garlic, minced
2 Tbsp olive oil
Red pepper flakes
1 Tbsp wheat-free tamari

Stack the collard greens and slice lengthwise in half.
Slice each stack into more bite-sized pieces, like 1-inch squares.
Heat 2 Tbsp olive oil in a large skillet or wok, add garlic and sauté until fragrant, about 30 seconds.
Add a dash of red pepper flakes and sauté another 10 seconds.
Add the collard greens and a splash of water (1 Tbsp).
Cook greens over medium heat until tender.
Stir in 1 Tbsp tamari before serving.

Gluten Free Noodle Kugel

This is a Jewish treat served at special holidays like Rosh Hashanah and Shavuot. It is usually loaded with cottage cheese, sour cream, and egg noodles, none of which are gluten free or dairy free. This one provides protein from eggs but contains no dairy and I've used Glutano Tagliatele to replace the egg noodles. The result was close enough to the traditional kugel that no one else would even know it was gluten-free!

1 pkg Glutano Tagliatele
2 eggs, preferably organic or free-range
1 can pineapple chunks, canned in juice, drained
1/3 cup raisins, dark or light
2-4 Tbsp Rapadura sugar (or organic brown sugar)*
1 Tbsp Rapadura sugar mixed with 1 tsp ground cinnamon*

Preheat oven to 350°.
Cook noodles according to package instructions.
Drain noodles and place in large bowl.
In a small bowl, beat eggs lightly with a fork.
Add eggs, drained pineapple, raisins, and sugar to noodles and mix thoroughly.
Lightly oil an 8 x 8 inch baking dish and fill with noodle mixture. Sprinkle with the sugar-cinnamon mixture.
Bake for about 1 hour or so.
*You can use maple sugar or date sugar instead of the Rapadura

Colcannon
Serves 4

A simple dish of mashed potatoes and greens, Colcannon is traditional Irish food, usually served on Halloween. Colcannon is usually made with either cabbage or kale; my recipe uses both. I have also added sautéed leeks (leeks and mashed potato is served in Ireland as a dish called "Champ") for extra flavor. Serve colcannon with something bright like roasted carrots or a carrot salad and some sliced apples or pears.

4-6 fist-sized potatoes (I like Yukon gold), cleaned and cut into chunks
4 cups shredded cabbage
4 cups kale, sliced into thin ribbons
2 leeks, well-cleaned, and sliced using only the white and light green parts
2 Tbsp olive oil
Salt and pepper

Preheat oven to 350°.
Bring a large saucepan of water to boil.
Add the potato chunks and cook over high heat until soft enough to stick a fork into. Remove potatoes with a slotted spoon and place them in a large bowl.
Continue to boil the water and add the cabbage and kale. Boil the vegetables for about 2-3 minutes until softened. Remove the vegetables but do not discard the cooking water.
Mash the potatoes, using 1 Tbsp olive oil and the potato cooking water, $\frac{1}{4}$ cup at a time.
Mix in the drained kale and cabbage.
Heat the remaining Tbsp olive oil in a skillet and sauté the leeks until golden.
Add these to the potato mixture.
Season to taste with salt and pepper.
Place the colcannon in a lightly oiled casserole and heat in the oven for about 10-15 minutes.
It is ok for it to be lightly browned on top.
Serve and enjoy.

Curried Tempeh Salad
Makes about 4 servings

Curried tempeh salad is tasty when served mounded on a bed of red leaf lettuce for a light summer meal or serve it as a high protein side dish to a light soup and salad any time of the year.

1 8oz package of tempeh (a gluten-free type)
$\frac{1}{2}$ cup grated carrot (about 2 medium)
Apple, unpeeled, $\frac{1}{2}$ cup diced
Onion, $\frac{1}{2}$ cup minced
$\frac{1}{4}$ cup raisins
1 Tbsp lemon or lime juice
1 Tbsp rice vinegar
$1\frac{1}{2}$ tsp agave nectar
$\frac{1}{4}$ cup vegan mayonnaise (gluten-free and dairy-free)
2 tsp curry powder
Lemon or lime zest from $\frac{1}{2}$ lemon or lime
2 Tbsp unsweetened shredded coconut or raw, dried, shredded coconut
$\frac{1}{2}$ cup raw unsalted cashews
2 Tbsp finely chopped cilantro

Cut the tempeh into small dice. Place in small saucepan with water to cover. Bring to a boil and then turn to simmer for 10 minutes. Drain the water and cool the tempeh.
While the tempeh is cooking, combine the grated carrot, diced apple, diced onion, and raisins in a bowl and toss with lemon or lime juice.
In a separate small bowl combine the rice vinegar, agave nectar, mayo and curry.
When the tempeh is cool, mash it slightly with the back of a fork, but leave some of the cubes whole. Add this to the carrot mixture and add the curry sauce. Toss everything well. Add the lime or lemon zest, coconut, cashews and cilantro and toss to combine.
Cover the bowl and refrigerate for at least an hour before serving.

Garlic Tofu with Bok Choy and Brown Rice
Serves 4 for dinner

Make the rice in the morning, and drain the tofu while chopping the other ingredients to make this meal faster to prepare. I generally find that tofu and vegetables are quick to cook and I often use this for nights when I have to make dinner at the last minute. Don't forget to use chopsticks for eating!

1 16oz package of extra firm tofu, drained
1 Tbsp canola oil
1 tsp canola oil
2 large cloves garlic, minced
2 Tbsp rice wine (mirin)
1 Tbsp wheat-free tamari (soy sauce)
1 tsp Agave nectar or honey
1 cup vegetable broth
2 Tbsp wheat-free Hoisin sauce (I use Premier Japan Organic Wheat-Free Hoisin Sauce)
1 tsp toasted sesame oil

Slice the tofu into 4 slices. Drain the slices on paper towel or a clean kitchen towel for 10 minutes.
Heat the Tbsp of canola oil in a large non-stick skillet.
Add the tofu and "fry" until golden brown, about 5 minutes on the first side, then 3-4 minutes on the second side.
Remove the tofu from the pan and set aside.
Heat 1 tsp canola oil in the skillet, add garlic and stir fry for about 30 seconds.
Add rice wine, soy sauce, Agave nectar, and broth. Bring this mixture to a boil, then add the tofu slices and cook over high heat until the tofu has absorbed most of the sauce.
Add the sesame oil and stir gently so you don't break the tofu pieces.

Bok Choy Stir Fry
1 Tbsp canola oil

1 small head of bok choy or ½ large cut lengthwise so there are both greens and stems, sliced, and separated into two piles, one for the white stems and one for the greens
1 cup green cabbage ribbons
½ medium onion, sliced lengthwise into half-moons
2 medium carrots, peeled and sliced diagonally into ¼inch thick slices
1/3 cup arame sea vegetable, soaked for 5 minutes in hot water (use the soaking water to fertilize your plants)
1 Tbsp mirin
1 Tbsp wheat-free tamari (soy sauce)
1 inch piece of fresh ginger, peeled and grated
1 tsp toasted sesame oil

Heat the oil in a large wok over high heat.
Add the onion, carrots, cabbage and bok choy stems. Cook over high heat, stirring constantly, about 3 minutes.
Drain the arame and add this to the stir fry. Stir to combine.
Add the mirin, soy sauce, and ginger.
Taste and season with a little more soy sauce if desired.
Finish the seasoning with the teaspoon of sesame oil and toss the mixture to integrate the oil. Remove from heat and serve.

<u>Brown Rice</u>
I often make dinner's brown rice in the morning while I am having breakfast which saves me time later in the day when I am more rushed to get dinner on the table. For 4 people I usually make 2 cups of dry brown rice with 4 cups water and will have leftover rice to use for lunch or for making one of the rice salads or the kale salad.

In a medium saucepan over medium high heat bring 2 cups rice and 4 cups water to a boil. Turn heat to low and cook until the water has been absorbed, 30-45 minutes. When the water is gone, turn off the heat, cover the pan and set it aside. The rice will continue to steam and get fluffier. Later, when you are ready to cook the rest of your meal, remove the cover, fluff the rice, and reheat in a covered dish in the oven.

Mushroom Stew
Serves 6

When I was growing up, my mom made a pot roast for special holidays that had a tomato-based sauce and lots of carrots and potatoes. Though even then I was not that interested in the meat, I loved the potatoes and carrots that had cooked for a long time in the sauce. I have tried to re-create mom's pot roast using "meaty" Portobello mushrooms. The result is comfort food for me and I hope you enjoy it as well. Serve the stew over quinoa-millet with a side of steamed Brussels sprouts.

2 Tbsp olive oil
5 Portobello mushroom caps, about 4 inches in diameter, rinsed and sliced into $\frac{1}{4}$-inch slices
2 onions, cut in half and sliced
3 carrots, peeled and sliced diagonally
2 fist-sized potatoes, peeled and cut into $\frac{1}{2}$ inch cubes
28-oz can diced tomatoes
1 bay leaf
$\frac{1}{4}$ cup tomato paste
$\frac{1}{4}$ tsp paprika
$\frac{1}{2}$ tsp each dried basil and oregano

In a large soup pot, heat the oil and add onion slices. Cook over medium heat until onions are soft.
Add the mushrooms and continue cooking until mushrooms begin to brown.
Add carrots, potatoes, tomatoes, bay leaf, tomato paste, paprika, basil, and oregano and stir to combine.
Cover pot and cook over medium-low heat for about 45 minutes until potatoes and carrots are soft enough to pierce with a fork.

Enjoy!

Greek Stuffed Peppers
Serves 4

In Greece stuffed peppers and tomatoes are found on the appetizer menu and it is customary to order several appetizers and call it dinner (which starts at 9:00 pm). The special ingredient here is the allspice, and pine nuts add a little extra toothsome texture.

4 large Bell peppers, red, green, or yellow
1 Tbsp olive oil
1 medium onion, chopped
1 tsp ground allspice
1 cup organic white rice
1 cup diced canned tomatoes
2 cups water
1/3 cup pine nuts, lightly toasted
¼ cup dark raisins
1 Tbsp oregano
½ cup chopped fresh parsley
2 Tbsp fresh lemon juice

Slice off the tops of the peppers and remove the seeds and white ribs. Invert onto paper towel to drain while you prepare the stuffing.

In a large skillet, heat 1 Tbsp olive oil and cook the onion until golden. Add allspice, rice, and tomatoes, stir to combine.

Add 2 cups water and bring to a boil. Turn heat to low simmer, cover the pan, and cook about 15 minutes. Turn off heat.

Add pine nuts and raisins and recover the pan until somewhat cooled. Stir in oregano and parsley.

Use the filling to stuff the peppers, mounding the filling on each one. You may have a little filling left which can be eaten for breakfast or lunch (or right away!).

Put the peppers in a glass baking dish or flat-bottomed casserole.

Drizzle the peppers with lemon juice.

Pour in about ½ cup water into the bottom of the pan and bake the peppers for 1 hour.

Italian Tofu Skillet Pasta
Serves 4 for dinner

Vegetarian ground meat substitutes are very convenient for adding to chili, stuffed peppers, and other vegetarian versions of dishes with meat. However, the meat substitutes that are currently available have wheat gluten, so people on gluten-free diets cannot use them. This dish uses tofu crumbles which are made by freezing and thawing the tofu, thus removing all the water; it is easy to put together for a weeknight meal but requires thinking ahead to make the tofu crumbles. Alternatively, you can press the tofu underneath heavy objects to drain the water, and crumble it into the skillet after sautéing the vegetables. Serve the pasta dish with a green salad.

1 lb firm or extra firm tofu made into tofu crumbles*
1 Tbsp olive oil
1 cup chopped onion
1 medium green pepper, diced
1 cup thinly sliced celery
2 cloves garlic, minced
1 16oz can diced tomatoes
2 cups tomato puree
$1\frac{1}{2}$ tsp oregano
$1\frac{1}{2}$ tsp basil
$\frac{1}{4}$ - $\frac{1}{2}$ tsp sea salt
Freshly ground pepper
$\frac{1}{2}$ lb gluten-free pasta (rice or rice & corn), cooked and drained

In a large skillet, heat the olive oil and add onion, green pepper, celery, and garlic and sauté for 3-4 minutes until vegetables are soft.
Add tofu crumbles and cook for another 2 minutes.
Add tomato puree, diced tomatoes, oregano and basil, and cook for another 2 minutes until fully combined.
Add cooked pasta and fold into the sauce so all is well combined.
Season with $\frac{1}{4}$ tsp salt and freshly ground pepper.

Taste the mixture to determine if the second ¼ tsp salt is needed.

* To prepare tofu crumbles:
Open a package of extra firm tofu and drain the liquid.
Place the tofu in a plastic bag and freeze for about 24 hours.
Remove the tofu from the freezer and thaw completely. The color is not as white as the fresh tofu.
With your hands, squeeze the water out of the thawed tofu. What you are left with is tofu that can be shredded or crumbled.

Make Your Own Taco Bar
Serves 4

<u>Bowls of</u>:
1 can fat-free vegetarian refried beans, placed in oven-proof baking dish and heated in oven at 350° until hot all the way through
1 can black beans, drained and rinsed
Chopped fresh tomato (about 1 cup, diced)
Chopped red onion (about ½ cup, diced)
Chopped red or green pepper (1 pepper, diced)
Shredded carrot (1 carrot, shredded)
Chopped lettuce (about 2 cups)
Chopped cilantro (about ¾ cup)
Josh's Guacamole (see *Dressings and Sauces*) or chopped avocado (guacamole is a wonderful substitute for sour cream, healthier and more flavorful too)
Salsa (your favorite homemade or bottled)
Shredded vegan cheese (optional)
Tofu sour cream (optional) (see *Dressings and Sauces*)
Gluten-free Corn tortillas (Food For Life) or taco shells

Place colorful bowls of vegetables, beans, and salsa in serving area. Allow family members to start with a corn tortilla or taco shell and fill it with any combination of beans, herbs, vegetables, and salsa.

Lentil Pilaf

This is another simple, Greek-inspired recipe. Serve the pilaf with a colorful carrot salad or orange vegetable like butternut squash.

4 Tbsp olive oil
1 onion, chopped
1 Tbsp ground coriander
$\frac{1}{2}$ tsp ground allspice
3 bay leaves
3 large carrots, quartered lengthwise and cut into 1 inch lengths
1 cup organic white rice
$\frac{3}{4}$ cup lentils
2 cups vegetable broth or water
Sea salt to taste
1 Tbsp honey
1 Tbsp red wine vinegar
3 Tbsp parsley
1 Tbsp oregano

Heat 2 Tbsp oil and sauté onion until soft.
Add spices and carrots and cook until carrots are coated and slightly softened, about 5 minutes.
Add rice and cook until rice is well coated with oil and spices.
Add lentils, broth and salt.
Bring to a boil and cook until liquid has disappeared, about 10 minutes.
Turn off heat and cover with a lid and let this sit for about 30 minutes.
Combine honey and vinegar and 2 Tbsp oil and warm.
Add parsley and oregano.
Turn the rice out into a serving bowl and pour the honey mixture over the rice.

Lentil-Olive Pasta Sauce

This is a chunky and hearty sauce which turns pasta into a
high-fiber, filling meal. Serve the sauce over brown rice pasta
with a sprinkle of nutritional yeast. For a weight and health-
conscious portion, serve only ½-1 cup of the pasta with plenty
of the sauce. For variation, the sauce is also delicious over
polenta. See my notes about polenta preparation (*Polenta &
Greens Supper*).

1 Tbsp olive oil
1 medium onion, cut in half and sliced lengthwise into half-
moons
4 cloves garlic, chopped
2 cups sliced mushrooms (1/2 of a 10-oz package)
1 cup shredded carrot
½ cup Kalamata olives, quartered
8 oz can tomato sauce
6 oz can tomato paste
2 ½ cups water
½ cups lentils
1½ tsp basil
1 tsp oregano
1 bay leaf
¼ tsp red pepper flakes
Sea salt and freshly ground pepper to taste
Fresh parsley, chopped (optional)

In a large saucepan sauté onion, garlic, and mushrooms in oil
until onion and mushrooms are soft.
Add carrot and sauté another 2 minutes to soften.
Add tomato sauce, tomato paste, water, lentils, olives, basil,
oregano, red pepper flakes and bay leaf and bring to boil.
Reduce heat to simmer, cover and cook for 35 minutes until
lentils are tender.
If desired, toss in ¼ cup chopped fresh parsley before serving.

Rice & Chard Pilaf
Serve 4

Here is another Greek-inspired meal that my tasters really loved. Serve with a colorful salad such as beets or carrot, and *Greek Lentil-Olive Spread* with rice crackers.

1 large onion, chopped
2 Tbsp extra virgin olive oil
2 cloves garlic, finely minced
1/8 tsp ground cumin
2 lbs Swiss chard, washed thoroughly, stalks removed, and chopped
¼ cup finely chopped fresh dill; (1 Tbsp dried)
1 cup organic white rice
2¼ cups vegetable broth
2 Tbsp fresh lemon juice
1-2 Tbsp extra virgin olive oil
Sea salt
Freshly ground black pepper
¼ cup pine nuts, lightly toasted

Heat the 2 Tbsp extra virgin olive oil in a large skillet. Add onion and sauté over medium heat until soft (2-3 minutes). Add garlic and cumin and cook for 1 minute.
Add the chard and toss periodically until chard is wilted, about 1-2 minutes.
Add the rice and mix thoroughly with chard.
Add vegetable broth and bring to a boil.
Simmer for about 10 minutes until liquid appears to be gone.
Add the dill, toss well and turn off heat.
Lay a clean kitchen towel over the rice mixture and cover the pan. Leave the pan for 30 minutes.
When you are ready to serve, remove the lid and towel, and pour the lemon juice and 1-2 Tbsp olive oil over the pilaf.

Toss to mix. Season with sea salt and pepper.
Garnish with toasted pine nuts and serve.

Smoked Tofu
4 servings

There are different flavors of smoked tofu available commercially but most have tamari which is not wheat-free. Use smoked tofu diced onto salads, diced into pasta salad, or added to tacos.

1 16-oz package of extra firm tofu
1 Tbsp water
2 Tbsp wheat-free tamari
1 Tbsp canola oil
2 tsp hickory smoke
1 tsp honey or maple syrup
$\frac{1}{4}$ tsp onion powder
$\frac{1}{4}$ tsp garlic powder
$\frac{1}{4}$ tsp thyme

Drain the tofu and slice in half so that you have 2 pieces of tofu the original length and width but thinner in thickness. Press the tofu for 30 minutes (see *Kale Salad* on page 100 for directions) before going to the next step.
In a small bowl, combine the water, tamari, canola oil, hickory smoke, honey or maple syrup, onion powder, garlic powder, and thyme.

Place the tofu slices in a shallow baking dish and pour the marinade over them, turning the tofu to coat all sides.
Marinate for 8 hours or overnight.
If possible, turn the tofu slices once or twice during the marinating time.
Place the baking dish with tofu and marinade in a 400° oven and bake for 30-45 minutes until liquid is absorbed, and tofu is firm.

Remove from oven and cool. The tofu will increase in firmness as it cools.

Rice Wrapper Egg Rolls
12 Egg Rolls

These egg rolls are delicious but probably not a weeknight meal since they are a little more labor intensive than most other recipes in this book. If you have help to make them, they go rather quickly. Serve the egg rolls with *Basic Miso Soup* and a green salad with *Carrot-Miso Dressing*. Note: there is very little allergy information about rice wrappers. If you are very gluten-sensitive or have celiac disease, these may not be for you.

2 Tbsp canola oil
2 stalks celery
1 small onion
2 cloves garlic
1 green pepper
1 cup sliced mushrooms, about 6 medium
2 cups green cabbage ribbons (or use pre-shredded coleslaw mix)
2 cups fresh mung bean sprouts
4 oz tempeh, grated
2 Tbsp wheat-free tamari
1 Tbsp mirin (rice wine)
1 tsp toasted sesame oil
12 rice wrappers (Spring roll wrappers)

In a food processor fitted with the steel blade, pulse the celery, onion, garlic, and pepper until finely chopped but not pureed.
Heat oil in a wok or other large pan, add vegetables from the food processor and cook over medium high heat for about 3 minutes until softened.
Add mushrooms and cook for another two minutes.
If mixture begins to stick to the bottom of the wok, add water, 1 Tbsp at a time, to moisten the vegetables.
Add cabbage and bean sprouts and cook for another two minutes until wilted.

Add tempeh, tamari, and mirin, and cook until tempeh is heated through and tamari and mirin are well distributed. Turn off heat.

Add sesame oil and mix well.

To assemble the egg rolls:

Place a large bowl of very hot water near your work space. You will also need a clean kitchen towel.

With a pair of tongs, hold a rice wrapper under the water for 7 seconds.

Remove the rice wrapper and place it on the towel for 2 minutes to soften.

Repeat with two more rice wrappers.

After two minutes, fill the first wrapper with 1/3 cup of the vegetable mixture by placing the mixture about 1$\frac{1}{2}$ inches in from one side of the wrapper.

Make the roll by folding top and bottom over the mixture, then the side.

Roll this until the whole wrapper has been used. It is like rolling a burrito.

Repeat with remaining vegetable mixture and rice wrappers.

To "fry" the egg rolls

In a large non-stick skillet, heat 1 Tbsp canola oil over medium heat. Add as many egg rolls as you can fit, while still being able to turn them over and move them around in the pan to evenly brown them.

Cook until nicely browned on all sides. Hold cooked rolls in the oven on a baking tray until ready to serve.

Simple Vegetable Stir Fry with Sea Vegetable
4-6 large portions

This is what I like to serve when I haven't planned anything
and I have to get dinner on the table quickly. I've been known
to *run* into the house, and, without taking off my coat, start
the brown rice which takes the longest to cook in a stir-fry
dinner. I almost always have tofu in the refrigerator so a meal
consisting of brown rice, skillet tofu, and a stir-fry of
whatever vegetables I have on hand is an easy last- minute
meal. You can use any combination of vegetables that you may
have. Besides what I have listed below, try mushrooms,
broccoli, cauliflower, spinach, cabbage, bok choy, edamame,
scallions. We always serve this with chopsticks.

1 red Bell pepper
2 medium carrots
1 stalk celery
8 oz snow peas
$\frac{1}{2}$ onion
$\frac{1}{2}$ cup arame sea vegetable, soaked for 5 minutes in cold water
(remember to save soaking water to use for watering some
nutrients into your house plants) and then drained
1 Tbsp canola, corn, or peanut oil
2 Tbsp wheat-free soy sauce
1 Tbsp mirin
1 Tbsp fresh ginger, minced
1 tsp toasted sesame oil
1 Tbsp raw sesame seeds

Brown rice
Tofu cooked your favorite easy way

Wash and chop all vegetables into separate bowls before
beginning to cook.
Cut pepper in half and slice each half (on the cut-side) into
thin strips.
Slice the carrots diagonally into 1/8-inch wide slices.
Slice the celery crosswise into thin slices.

134

Leave the snow peas whole or slice in half diagonally to make more manageably-sized pieces.
Cut the onion half in ½ again.
Place each quarter cut-side down, and slice thinly.
This creates nice half-moon slivers of onion.
Heat the canola oil in a large wok over high heat.
Add onion and stir-fry for about 30 seconds.
Add carrots and celery and cook for 1 minute.
Add pepper and snow peas and cook for another minute.
Turn down heat to medium.
Add pre-soaked arame and toss to combine, still cooking.
Add soy sauce, mirin, and ginger and toss until vegetables are coated.
Add sesame oil and seeds, toss to combine, and remove from heat.

Serve the vegetables along with brown rice and tofu cooked your favorite way.
Eat with chopsticks.

Tempeh Bacon BLT
Makes about 8-10 slices

Tempeh bacon can be purchased under the name of Fakin' Bacon by LightLife. Unfortunately, the tamari soy sauce used is not wheat-free so it is not a gluten-free food. My family tried 3 different recipes for our own homemade tempeh bacon and this was the one we liked best! Enjoy tempeh bacon on toasted gluten-free bread with crisp Romaine lettuce, sliced tomato, and gluten-free mayonnaise. It is also delicious on a sandwich with *Tofu Eggless Salad* (Snacks). Vegans and those with egg allergy can use an egg-free mayo. Tempeh bacon is also good on a salad or used in any recipe that requires a smoky-flavored meat.

Marinade
$\frac{1}{4}$ cup water
$\frac{1}{4}$ cup wheat-free soy sauce
1 Tbsp canola oil
1 Tbsp honey or pure maple syrup
1 Tbsp liquid hickory smoke
$\frac{3}{4}$ tsp onion powder
$\frac{3}{4}$ tsp garlic powder
1 8oz package of gluten-free tempeh (soy, vegetable, flax, or wild rice type)

Stir together marinade ingredients and place in 6" x 12" baking dish.
Cut tempeh lengthwise into 8-10 long strips.
Place tempeh strips in marinade and toss gently to coat.
Marinate 8 hours or overnight.
Place marinated strips on greased baking sheet with a lip (jellyroll pan), pour remaining marinade over strips and bake at 400° until liquid is almost gone and tempeh is nicely browned, turning once during the baking (halfway through).
This takes about 20 minutes.

A few words on tempeh..........................

Tempeh, which has long been an Indonesian staple food, is made from fermented soybeans. It is a great source of soy protein, with 22 grams of protein, 250 calories, 14 grams of fiber, and 10 grams of fat in $\frac{1}{2}$ of an 8 oz package. This amount of protein is equivalent to the number of grams of protein in 3 oz of animal protein (meat, fish or poultry). Tempeh is a complete protein containing all of the essential amino acids and 100 grams of tempeh offers 1.0 microgram vitamin B12 which is very important and can be difficult to get in a vegan diet. Be careful and read labels. Tempeh has additional ingredients ranging from gluten-containing grains to just vegetables. The four flavors I have found that are gluten-free tempeh are: wild rice, soy, flax, and vegetable. If in doubt, call the company to confirm the ingredients.

Tempeh Fajitas
Serves 4 for dinner

In my house we love any food with Mexican flavors. Fajitas always smell so good in restaurants. Here is our vegetarian version. The tempeh is first marinated and then baked. If the spices are not enough for you, they are easily multiplied.

1 8-oz pkg of gluten-free tempeh

Marinade
2 Tbsp canola oil
2 Tbsp gluten-free soy sauce
1 Tbsp tomato paste
1 Tbsp maple syrup
1 tsp chili powder
½ tsp each ground cumin and oregano
¼ tsp garlic powder

1 stack of corn tortillas (gluten-free)
2 large red Bell peppers
2 large onions
1 Tbsp olive oil
2 tsp ground cumin
2 tsp ground chili powder
1 tsp garlic powder
1/2 tsp onion powder
1 jar of your favorite salsa
  (my personal favorite is pico de gallo)

Josh's Guacamole (Dressings and Sauces)
Tofu Sour Cream (Dressings and Sauces)

Cut the tempeh crosswise in half, then cut each half into 10 pieces ½ inch by 3 inches, and ¼ inch thick.
Combine the ingredients for the marinade in a 9x13 pan.
Add the tempeh and roll each piece to coat with marinade.
Marinate for at least an hour or more, periodically turning over the pieces of tempeh to coat them.

138

Preheat the oven to 350°.
Combine 2 tsp cumin, 2 tsp chili powder, 1 tsp garlic powder, and ½ tsp onion powder on a plate.
Dredge the tempeh pieces to coat them with the spices and place on an oiled baking pan.
Bake the strips for 20 minutes, turning them halfway through the baking.

While the tempeh is baking, slice the peppers into strips and set aside. Cut the onions in half crosswise. Slice each onion half in two, cutting through the root end and slice them into long thin pieces including a piece of the root end with each slice. Heat the oil in a large skillet and add the onions and peppers. Cook over medium high heat until soft. It is fine if they get brown, in fact, they taste much better if they do. Alternatively, you can grill the onions and peppers in a grill basket; this takes about 30 minutes over a medium heat. While the tempeh is baking and the onions and peppers are cooking, soften the tortillas by brushing each one lightly with oil and heating in a large skillet, one or two at a time, for a minute or two, turning them over halfway through. Don't overcook or they will be crispy and break when you try to fill them.

To assemble a fajita, place 2 or 3 tempeh strips, a forkful of the peppers and onions, a dab of salsa, and a dab each of guacamole and tofu sour cream in a tortilla, roll, and eat.

Tofu Scramble

Serves 1 and easily multiplied to serve any number

This is one of my favorite breakfasts! The tofu provides low fat protein and you begin your day with one or two servings of vegetables already "under your belt". I always start with an onion and I almost always have mushrooms and celery on hand. After that, there are lots of variations with leftover cooked vegetables and different spice combinations. Try some of my suggestions and then feel free to create your own!

1/5 package of extra firm tofu, cut into cubes; start by cutting the tofu block into five pieces
1-3 fresh mushrooms, washed and sliced
1 small onion or $\frac{1}{4}$ large, roughly chopped
1 plum tomato, roughly chopped
$\frac{1}{2}$ stalk celery, diced
$\frac{1}{4}$ green pepper, diced
Leftover veggies: broccoli, asparagus, cauliflower, potato, cooked carrot, snow peas, spinach, peas, corn (especially corn cut from leftover corn-on-the-cob), about $\frac{1}{2}$ cup chopped
Canola or olive oil
Seasonings as below

In a lightly oiled large skillet or non-stick pan, sauté the onion and mushrooms for 2 minutes over medium high heat.
Add tofu, tomato, celery, pepper and other vegetables and continue sautéing for another 3 minutes, using a spatula to toss the vegetables around the pan. Add any leftover vegetables and continue to cook until heated through.
For a Tex-Mex flavor, add a sprinkle of chili powder and ground cumin when you sauté the onion. If you have any chipotle chili, a tsp of this adds a great smoky hot flavor. If you have any cilantro, add a couple of tablespoons chopped. Serve with a corn tortilla if desired. Or you can sprinkle with tortilla confetti (see *South of the Border Soup with Tortilla Confetti* in the Main Dish section) for an extra crunch.

For an Asian taste use broccoli, asparagus, and snow peas, and add 1 Tbsp wheat-free soy sauce, chopped scallions, and finish with $\frac{1}{2}$ tsp toasted sesame oil.

A more Indian combination would be some ground cumin, ground coriander, and turmeric. Again, add the spices when you sauté the onion.

Polenta & Greens Supper
Serves 4 as main dish

Polenta is vegetarian comfort food! The corn grits used in this recipe give a wonderful chewy texture which will convert even skeptics into polenta lovers. Try any combination of these additions: pre-soaked chopped sun dried tomatoes, chopped Kalamata olives, minced rosemary or basil, sautéed mushrooms. Serve the polenta with *Garlic Kale* or other green vegetable, and something orange such as *Moroccan Carrot Salad.*

$4\frac{1}{2}$ cups water
$1\frac{1}{2}$ cups organic corn grits (I use Neshaminy Valley or Bob's Red Mill)*
1 tsp ghee (optional)
1 Tbsp extra virgin olive oil
Sea salt and freshly ground black pepper to taste

In a medium saucepan bring the water to boil, add the polenta, and stir with a wire whisk.
Turn the heat to medium and cook for about 20 minutes until polenta is very thick.
If you are using any additions, stir them in at this point.
The polenta will continue to thicken as it cools.
Cool slightly and serve.

*Note: this is truly wonderful with the coarse corn grits and worth the effort of finding them. The grits in the recipe are NOT the Quaker brand of grits used for morning cereal.

Vegetable Lasagna with Tofu Ricotta
Makes a 9x13 inch pan

This lasagna is made in a 9x13 pan and uses a whole box of lasagna noodles. Overlap the noodles in the pan and make sure to place a noodle at the short end so that the whole pan is covered.

1 box gluten-free lasagna noodles
    (I use Tinkyada Brown Rice noodles)
6 oz tomato paste
$15\frac{1}{2}$ oz flavorful tomato sauce
    (your favorite, without additives)
2 cups water
1 Tbsp olive oil
1 onion, chopped
10 oz mushrooms, sliced
8 oz carrots, grated
8 oz fresh spinach, washed thoroughly and chopped coarsely
$\frac{1}{4}$ cup chopped Kalamata olives

Tofu Ricotta
1 lb water-packed extra firm tofu, drained
1 Tbsp yellow miso
2 Tbsp olive oil
2 large cloves garlic
1 Tbsp lemon juice
2 tsp basil
2 tsp oregano
$\frac{1}{4}$ tsp sea salt

Preheat oven to 375°.
Cook the lasagna noodles according to package directions.
Drain the water and lay the noodles out on a clean towel or waxed paper for later use.
Combine the tomato paste, tomato sauce, and 2 cups water in a saucepan. Combine using a wire whisk.

In a large skillet heat 1 Tbsp olive oil.
Add onion and mushrooms and cook until softened.
Add carrots and spinach and cook until carrots are soft and spinach has wilted, about 2-3 minutes.
Turn off heat and stir in the olives.
Set this vegetable mixture aside.

Make the tofu ricotta
Place all ingredients in food processor and pulse until fully combined.
Process for a few seconds until the mixture is smooth.

Putting the lasagna together.
Place 1 cup of the sauce in the bottom of your 9x13 pan. Add noodles in 1 layer, overlapping the edges slightly, to cover the bottom of the pan.
Place dollops of the tofu ricotta over the noodles, using about half.
Place dollops of the vegetable mixture over the tofu ricotta, using about half.
Pour about 1 cup remaining sauce over the lasagna and top with more noodles.
Repeat steps with remaining tofu ricotta and vegetable mixture.
Top with another cup of the sauce and then remaining noodles.
Pour all of the rest of the sauce on the noodles.
Bake the lasagna uncovered for about 45 minutes .
Let the lasagna rest for 10 minutes before cutting.

Buon appetito!

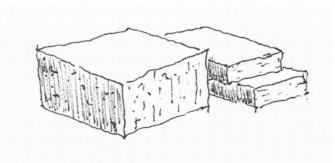

White Bean Stuffed Portobello Mushrooms Over Spring Greens with Polenta Croutons
Serves 4

The filling for these stuffed mushroom caps is a savory white bean spread with garlic and rosemary. You may or may not use all of the filling depending on the size of the mushroom caps. If you have any leftover filling, it is a great spread on celery sticks or rice crackers. The recipe is easily multiplied by the number of people you have.

4 Portobello mushroom caps, 5-inch diameter, stems removed, marinated for at least 1 hour in **Maple Mustard Vinaigrette** (Dressings and Sauces)
1 14-16 oz can small white beans (not white kidney beans), drained and rinsed
2 garlic cloves, any size, large if you love garlic
2 tsp olive oil
2 Tbsp water
2 plum tomatoes, cut in half, then each half cut into four, then cut across into dice
¼ cup chopped curly parsley
¼ cup minced red onion (about 2 large slices of an onion)
1 tsp finely chopped fresh rosemary
Salt and pepper
Olive oil for drizzling

Salad
1 package of organic spring mix greens
1 garlic clove
Olive oil
1 Tbsp fresh lemon juice
Salt and pepper

Cooked polenta (optional) (see *Polenta & Greens Supper*)*
Preheat oven to 450°. Spray a baking sheet lightly with oil. Roast the mushrooms for about 10 minutes, then turn and roast for another 10 minutes. Remove from oven.

Meanwhile, prepare the filling. In a food processor place the beans, garlic, 2 tsp olive oil, and 2 Tbsp water. Process until a paste has been formed.

Remove bean mixture to a small bowl and add a sprinkle of salt and pepper, chopped parsley, and rosemary. Stir to combine. Fill each mushroom cap with bean mixture, mounding slightly. Top each cap with 1 Tbsp chopped tomato and 1 tsp chopped onion. Sprinkle with salt and pepper and drizzle each cap with a small amount of olive oil (about $\frac{1}{2}$ tsp or less).

Broil for about 4-5 minutes until warm.

To prepare salad

In a large salad bowl measure olive oil, 1 tsp per person. Press the garlic clove through a garlic crusher into the oil and stir to incorporate. Add greens and toss with a large fork until leaves are coated with oil.

Sprinkle with salt and pepper and toss again.

Note: Save this last part until right before serving. When you are ready to serve, add the lemon juice to the salad and toss. Pile salad on each plate and place the mushroom cap on top. Serve with warm squares of polenta or "polenta croutons". To make the croutons, cut the polenta into cubes and sauté these in a skillet until lightly browned. If using croutons, place the salad in the middle of the plate with the mushroom cap in the center and scatter the polenta croutons randomly.

*You can follow the recipe in this book (*Polenta & Greens Supper*). After cooking the polenta, spoon it into a 9x13 inch baking dish and smooth the top. Refrigerate until very firm. Cut into squares and reheat under the broiler, on the grill, or in a skillet with some olive oil. For a deep-dish polenta, use a 6x12 inch baking dish.

Tofu-Broccoli Stuffed Potatoes
Serves 4

Tasty even without cheese! Once the potatoes are baked, it goes together quickly. To save time, try baking the potatoes in the morning while you're having breakfast and leave them to cool until you come home. Serve with a colorful salad.

4 large baking potatoes, about 6-9 oz each
2 cups broccoli florets, lightly steamed but still bright green
10 oz firm tofu, drained (please weigh to get the right amount)
2 large cloves garlic
2 Tbsp nutritional yeast
2 Tbsp olive oil
¼ cup unsweetened soymilk
Sea salt and freshly ground pepper to taste

Preheat the oven to 450°.
Scrub the potatoes and make a small 1-inch puncture with a knife in each one. Bake the potatoes about 1 hour until they give when you squeeze them. Remove from the oven and let cool enough that you can handle them.
Slice off a thin piece of the top of each potato.
Set these pieces aside; they are a snack for the cook or someone passing through the kitchen.
Using a spoon, carefully scrape out the potato into a large bowl, leaving the shell to be re-stuffed.
Press the garlic cloves through a garlic press into the bowl with the potatoes. Add the olive oil and soy milk and mash all together. Crumble the tofu into the mashed potatoes and stir in. Add the steamed broccoli, 1 Tbsp nutritional yeast, salt, and pepper and mix together.
Heat the oven to 400°.
Stuff the potato mixture into each potato and set them in a flat-bottomed baking dish. Mound as much potato mixture on top of each potato as possible; any that is left over can be eaten for lunch the next day.
Sprinkle the potatoes with 1 Tbsp nutritional yeast.
Bake for 20 minutes until very hot.

Simple Vegetable Sides

Broccoli Raab

I used to cook my broccoli raab without blanching until I ate it in Rome. Blanching removes some of the bitterness and allows the olive oil to really soak in. I like it much better this way. Leftover cooked broccoli raab is *delicious* on a hummus sandwich!

1 bunch broccoli raab
2-3 garlic cloves, minced
½ tsp red pepper flakes
1-2 Tbsp extra virgin olive oil
Sea salt to taste

Wash the broccoli raab and remove the woody stems, about 2 inches of the bottom.
Cut the vegetable across to make 4-inch lengths.
In a large soup pot bring 10 cups of water to boil.
Drop the broccoli raab in the water and turn down heat to medium high.
Cook 3 minutes.
Remove broccoli raab immediately from water, drain, and place in a bowl until ready to cook with the garlic and oil.
Drain the water from the soup pot.
Right before you are ready to serve heat 1 Tbsp olive oil in a large skillet.
Sauté the garlic for about 30 seconds until fragrant but not brown.
Add the red pepper flakes and stir for a few seconds.
Add the broccoli raab and stir to cover the leaves with the garlic and oil.
Drizzle with the 2nd Tbsp olive oil and toss to distribute.
Sprinkle with sea salt to taste.

Grilled Vegetables

Grilled vegetables are wonderful hot the first day, or cold the next day on your lunch salad. If you have a simple-to-use gas grill, you can have grilled vegetables even in the dead of winter (if you're willing to run back and forth to the grill with your coat on).

10 oz box mushrooms
2 large red or green peppers
2 large onions
3 Tbsp olive oil
1 tsp garlic powder
$\frac{1}{2}$ tsp oregano
$\frac{1}{2}$ tsp basil
Salt/pepper

Wash mushrooms, slice in half or quarters if they are large, and place in large bowl.
Slice peppers into wide slices or 1 inch squares.
Add to bowl.
Cut onions in half and then slice the halves lengthwise into slivers.
Toss vegetables with olive oil, garlic powder, oregano, basil and salt and pepper.

Grill about 25-30 minutes, stirring every 5-10 minutes.

If desired, toss with 1 Tbsp Balsamic vinegar.
If you like, you can add chunks of zucchini.

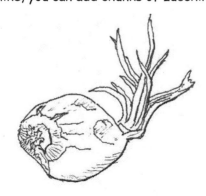

Kale with Garlic and Olive Oil

Blanching kale before cooking it with oil and garlic removes the bitterness. Kale is highly alkalizing to the body and packed with nutrients.

1 bunch fresh kale (about $\frac{3}{4}$ lb)
2 large cloves garlic
2 Tbsp olive oil (preferably extra virgin)
1-2 tsp fresh lemon juice
1/8 tsp sea salt

Wash the kale thoroughly and remove the leaves from the stems by tearing them off into small pieces.
Place the pieces in a large bowl or colander.
In a large soup pot bring 10 cups of water to boil.
Drop the kale in the water and turn down heat to medium high.
Cook 4 minutes.
Remove kale immediately from water, drain, and place in a bowl until ready to cook with the garlic and oil.
Drain the water from the soup pot.
Right before you are ready to serve heat 1 Tbsp olive oil in the same pot you used to blanch the kale.
Sauté the garlic for about 30 seconds until fragrant but not brown.
Add the kale and stir to cover the leaves with the garlic and oil.
Turn off heat.
Sprinkle the kale with salt and lemon juice and toss well to distribute.
Drizzle the kale with the 2nd Tbsp olive oil and toss to distribute.

Serve.

Roasted Cauliflower & Broccoli

Roasting is a very easy way to prepare vegetables, particularly if you buy the fresh broccoli already in florets. I can get a 3 lb bag of broccoli florets and about 2 lbs will fit comfortably in my roasting pan. I usually make a lot and snack on the leftovers.

1 Tbsp olive oil per pound of broccoli or cauliflower
Fresh broccoli or cauliflower florets

Preheat oven to 500°.
Place 2 lbs broccoli florets in a large roasting pan. Toss with 2 Tbsp olive oil.
Roast for 20 minutes until lightly browned.
Remove from oven. Lightly salt and pepper if desired.

For cauliflower, follow same directions as above.
Add 1 Tbsp fresh or dried rosemary, or other herb if preferred.

Spaghetti Squash

What a fun vegetable. Long spaghetti-like strands of squash that you can dress any way you like. Add it to stir-frys, top with Lentil Olive Pasta Sauce or your favorite marinara.

Preheat oven to 350° and lightly oil a shallow baking pan such as a jelly-roll pan.
Start with a nice looking spaghetti squash of any size.
Cut your squash in half and scoop out the seeds.
Place the halves cut-side down on the baking pan.
Bake the squash until it is tender and you can stick a fork into it, about an hour.
Remove from the oven and cool until you can hold the squash.
Using a fork, pull the threads of squash into a bowl.
Top with sauce and enjoy!

Roasted Roots
Serves 4 as a side dish with leftovers

It is important that your cut vegetables be somewhat uniform in size so that they cook in the same amount of time. If they are all different sizes, you will have some very soft vegetables and overly firm vegetables. You can substitute 1 Tbsp dried crumbled sage leaves (not ground) instead of the rosemary or try other herbs that you like. This is a side dish that can be served with a tofu or tempeh main dish. Leftovers taste great on your lunch salad the next day.

3 cups peeled and cubed rutabaga
2 cups peeled and cubed sweet potato
1 large parsnip, peeled and sliced
2 small turnips, peeled and cubed
2 Tbsp olive oil
$\frac{1}{4}$ cup vegetable broth
Sea salt and freshly ground pepper to taste
1 -2 Tbsp fresh rosemary if you have it, or 1 Tbsp dried rosemary (optional)

Preheat oven to 400°.
Lightly oil a large roasting pan.
Place all vegetables in the pan and toss with 2 Tbsp olive oil until well coated.
If you are using the rosemary, add it and toss well.
Sprinkle vegetable broth over the vegetables.
Lightly salt and pepper.
Cover with foil for the first 15 minutes of roasting.
Roast for about 45 minutes until vegetables are tender but not mushy.

Sweet Potatoes Baked, Grilled, Roasted

Sweet potatoes are a powerhouse food loaded with vitamin A and potassium. They are also alkalizing to the body. I love sweet potatoes almost any way they can be made. Here are three simple ways to cook sweet potatoes without loading them up with sugar or marshmallows.

Baked
1 medium sized sweet potato per person

Preheat oven to 400°.
Wash sweet potatoes and poke a few holes with a fork.
They tend to "leak" sticky juices all over the oven so I like to use a baking sheet.
Bake on a baking sheet for about 1 hour or until they can be squeezed (tender).
Serve them in their jackets as is.

Grilled
1 medium sized sweet potato per person
1-2 Tbsp olive oil

Preheat your grill.
Peel sweet potatoes and cut into fries.
Toss in a bowl with olive oil.
Spray a large piece of tin foil with oil.
Wrap sweet potato fries in the foil, allowing room around the vegetables for steam to help them cook.
Place the foil package on the grill and close the cover.
They take 30-45 minutes.
Be careful when you open the foil to see if they are tender, the steam is very hot and can burn.

Roasted
If you don't have a grill or don't feel like trekking through the snow to get to it, roasted sweet potatoes are for you.

1 medium sized sweet potato per person
1-2 Tbsp olive oil

Preheat the oven to 400°.
Peel the sweet potatoes and cut into 1-inch chunks.
Toss with olive oil in a bowl and transfer to roasting pan.
Roast for about 45 minutes until tender and lightly browned.

Note: Try adding some cumin and chili powder before roasting or grilling.

Asparagus with Olive Oil

This is very simple and really allows the flavor of the vegetable to come through. We like ours still a little crispy. If you do not have or like to use a microwave you may steam the asparagus.

1 bunch fresh asparagus
1 Tbsp extra virgin olive oil
Sea salt

Trim off the woody ends of the asparagus.
Place in a microwave-safe dish with 1 Tbsp water and cover with waxed paper.
Microwave for 3-4 minutes until the asparagus are bright green.
Drizzle with olive oil and use tongs to toss the asparagus with the oil.
Sprinkle with a little salt to taste.

Snacks

- Snacks should provide some nutrition, satisfy your hunger and taste good!

- Protein improves alertness and sustains your hunger.

- Carbohydrates provide energy. Whole grains are filling carbohydrates that have an even impact on your blood sugar; fruits and vegetables have a high nutrient impact, and plenty of fiber.

- Soup is good food, full of water, vegetables, lowfat carbohydrates like potatoes and brown rice, lowfat vegetarian proteins such as chickpeas, split peas or lentils. It is full of nutrition, warm and comforting, very filling, and great as a snack or a meal with salad and toasted gluten-free bread.

Try these ideas
- Vegetable sushi (use a wheat-free soy sauce & wasabi for dipping)
- Vegetable soup – homemade or low fat, gluten-free canned
- Nutritious dips/spreads like hummus or lentil spread with raw vegetables like low fat baby carrots, cucumber slices, celery sticks, peppers, fennel, or gluten-free crackers or rice cakes
- Bruschetta (fresh tomato/basil/garlic) with toasted gluten-free bread or your favorite gluten-free crackers. Try *Hannah's* brand Bruschetta
- Your favorite flavor soy yogurt, peeled orange cut into pieces, drizzle with 1 tsp honey and sprinkle with 1-2 tsp raw unsalted sunflower seeds
- Guacamole and low fat gluten-free tortilla chips
- Fresh apple, pear, or banana with 1 Tbsp natural (salted ok, no added sugar) peanut butter or almond butter

- Gluten-free multi-grain cereal (my favorite is Nature's Path Mesa Sunrise cereal with corn, flax, amaranth, buckwheat & quinoa) with soy milk and fresh berries or banana
- 1 cup hot rice cereal or grits, top with soy milk, 1 tsp raw sunflower seeds, 1 Tbsp raisins and/or fresh fruit such as chopped apple or banana
- Fruit and juice shake: $\frac{1}{2}$ cup orange or pineapple juice, $\frac{1}{2}$ banana or $\frac{1}{2}$ cup berries, $\frac{1}{2}$ cup vanilla soy yogurt or 1/3 cup lite silken tofu
- Soymilk and frozen fruit shake: 1 cup vanilla or chocolate soymilk (Silk), frozen banana or strawberries or raspberries
- Homemade fruit & cereal bar
- "Cottage cheese" toastie: 1 slice gluten-free toast, spread with $\frac{1}{4}$ cup mashed tofu mixed with 1 tsp maple syrup, sprinkle with cinnamon-date sugar and 1 tsp raw sunflower seeds or walnuts, top with sliced peaches or apple or banana, broil until "cheese" is bubbly but not burnt.
- Hot cocoa: In a mug place 2 tsp maple sugar and 2 heaping tsp unsweetened cocoa powder. Heat 1 cup soy milk in a glass measuring cup, pour into mug while stirring. Fat free and delicious!!!
- Homemade lowfat, rich, chocolatey soy pudding: whisk together $\frac{1}{4}$ cup maple sugar, $\frac{1}{4}$ cup unsweetened cocoa powder, 2 Tbsp cornstarch or tapioca starch and a pinch of salt in a 2-quart heavy saucepan and gradually whisk in 2 cups soy milk. Boil, whisking constantly until pudding is thick, 3-5 min. Pour into 6oz cups/bowls and cover with plastic wrap to prevent a skin from forming. Chill until set.
- Gluten-free waffles (Van's or another gluten-free brand or homemade) topped with fresh berries (or other fruit) and a dollop of your favorite flavor soy yogurt.
- Slice fruits such as banana, pineapple, orange, strawberries, apples, or pears. Warm some Wax

Orchards Fat Free Fruit-sweetened Fudge and dip the
fruit slices for a decadent snack or dessert.

Ceci Nuts

Ceci is Italian for chickpeas and the recipe comes from my
Italian friend John Pierro. The chickpeas are roasted for an
hour until crunchy and are delicious flavored only with olive oil,
salt, and pepper. I use 1 tsp oil per cup of chickpeas, so each
cup of roasted chickpeas ends up with about 150 calories, far
less calories and fat than $\frac{1}{2}$ cup of tree nuts would provide. I
offer you this simple recipe with a couple of spicy variations.
Mangia!

1 (14-16 oz) can chickpeas, rinsed, and drained
1 tsp coarse salt (Kosher or sea)
2 tsp olive oil
Freshly ground black pepper

Toss chickpeas with salt, pepper, and olive oil in a bowl.
Transfer to shallow baking dish or jelly-roll pan which has been
lightly sprayed with olive oil.
Bake at 400° for 1-1$\frac{1}{4}$ hrs, stirring occasionally.
They are done when the chickpeas are crispy.

Variation
2 cans chickpeas
1 Tbsp chili powder
1 tsp ground cumin
$\frac{1}{2}$ tsp garlic powder
1/8 tsp cayenne pepper
1 Tbsp olive oil

Banana Orange Animal-Free "Jello"
Easily multiplied

Agar Agar Flakes, known as Kanten in Japan, are made from sea vegetables with thickening properties and work much the way animal-based gelatin does. The Agar is added to juice or other liquid, heated to boiling, and then simmered about 5 minutes until fully dissolved. Then fruits are added and it is cooled. In a short time you have homemade "jello" without added sugar, color, chemical or animal, and which can be cut into shapes if desired. Try your own variations.

1 cup orange juice
Agave nectar to taste (optional)
1 banana
1 Tbsp Agar Agar Flakes sea vegetable

In a small serving bowl, slice the banana and arrange on the bottom of the bowl in an attractive pattern.
Place the juice in a small saucepan.
Sprinkle the Agar flakes over the juice.
Over medium heat, bring the juice and flakes to a boil.
Turn down heat to simmer and cook, stirring with a wire whisk, for about 5 minutes until the flakes are fully dissolved.
Pour the juice over the banana slices.
Chill the Kanten until firm.
Kanten can also be made in individual portions in 6oz ramekins.

Variations
Try using other juices like unsweetened apple juice or apricot nectar.
Try adding sliced strawberries, fresh blueberries, or orange slices.

Mandarin orange-kiwi-strawberry
Use 2 cups unsweetened organic apple juice, 1 Tbsp maple syrup, grated lemon rind from $\frac{1}{2}$ lemon, $1\frac{1}{2}$ Tbsp Agar flakes, 4 sliced strawberries, 2 peeled and sliced kiwis, and 1 can juice-packed Mandarin oranges.

Place all fruit in bottom of serving bowl.
Bring apple juice and Agar flakes to a boil, and then reduce heat to simmer and cook for 5 minutes.
Stir in lemon rind.
Pour juice over fruit. Refrigerate until firm.

Hummus
Makes about 2 cups

Hummus is a wonderful dip made of chickpeas, sesame paste (tahini), lemon juice, and garlic. Traditional recipes also have a lot of olive oil which makes them tasty but higher in calories and fat. My recipe eliminates the olive oil and uses only tahini for the fat. I think you'll agree it is much better than store-bought hummus! Serve hummus with rice cakes, rice crackers, or raw vegetables. Think out of the breakfast box a little and try hummus on gluten-free toast with sliced cucumber, tomato and alfalfa sprouts for breakfast.

1 14-oz can chickpeas, drained and rinsed
Juice of $\frac{1}{2}$ lemon
1 garlic clove
$\frac{1}{4}$ cup water
2 Tbsp sesame tahini
Sea salt to taste

In a food processor fitted with steel blade, process the garlic until minced.
Add the chickpeas and water and process until almost smooth.
Add the tahini and lemon juice and process until creamy.
Season lightly with sea salt.

For variety, add any of the following
Pre-soaked sun-dried tomatoes, fresh basil, pitted Kalamata olives (or your favorite olives), jalapeno pepper, roasted garlic, roasted red pepper, scallions

Cranberry Orange Walnut Bread
1 8"x4" loaf and 1 mini loaf

This variation on the Date Nut Bread (page 162) uses orange juice, gluten-free brown rice syrup, and maple syrup to sweeten. The bread is very dense with a great mix of flavors from the tart cranberries, the orange zest, and the walnuts. The texture is much heavier than cake-like cranberry bread but we think it is quite tasty.

$\frac{1}{2}$ cup dates, chopped or sliced
1 cup orange juice, heated until very hot
2 eggs
$\frac{1}{4}$ cup gluten-free brown rice syrup
$\frac{1}{4}$ cup pure maple syrup
$\frac{1}{4}$ cup canola oil
1 tsp vanilla extract
Grated zest of a whole orange
$2\frac{1}{4}$ cups gluten-free flour mix (I like to use 2 cups of gluten free flour mix and $\frac{1}{4}$ cup teff flour for the last $\frac{1}{4}$ cup)
2 tsp xanthan gum
1 Tbsp aluminum-free baking powder
1 tsp baking soda
$1\frac{1}{2}$ cups fresh cranberries, coarsely chopped
1 cup walnuts, coarsely chopped
Preheat oven to 350°.

Lightly oil an 8"x4" loaf pan and a mini loaf pan.
Place dates in a medium bowl, pour the cup of hot orange juice over them and allow them to sit for 30 minutes.
Meanwhile, beat eggs with mixer, add gluten-free brown rice syrup, maple syrup, oil and mix together.
Add vanilla, orange zest, xanthan gum, baking powder, and gluten-free flour mix and mix with beaters.
Remove beaters and stir in the dates-juice mixture, add the cranberries and walnuts and combine until no dry ingredients remain.
Pour the batter into the prepared pans.

Bake for 1 to 1¼ hours until lightly browned and a toothpick inserted into center comes out clean.

If there is a crevice running down the center or side of the bread, do not worry about this; it holds together if you wait several hours before slicing.

Let bread cool in pan for 10 minutes. Run knife around the edge and invert the bread onto a cooling rack or clean kitchen towel. Allow to fully cool for a few hours before attempting to slice; the bread will be more solid and less apt to crumble.

Use a serrated bread knife to slice this bread and if needed, turn the bread over and slice from the bottom to prevent crumbling.

Optional Glaze

You can make a glaze from 1 Tbsp gluten-free brown rice syrup mixed with 1 Tbsp orange juice.

Combine these well and then drizzle over the still-hot bread. Allow the bread to fully cool for a few hours before slicing.

Peach Shake

Add 1-2 Tbsp hemp protein powder for an extra boost of lean protein and omega-3's. Frozen blueberries (¼ - ½ cup) may be added to this shake; you will need to increase the amount of soymilk used. Try a Peach Melba variation by adding ¼-½ cup frozen raspberries.

½ cup frozen peaches with no added sugar
1 cup soymilk (vanilla is preferable, but plain will do)*
¼ tsp almond extract
Dash cardamom
Honey, agave nectar or maple syrup as needed to sweeten

Place all ingredients in the blender. Blend until smooth, adding more soymilk if needed. You may also sweeten further with honey, brown rice syrup, or maple syrup; add 1 Tbsp at a time.

*Rice milk, almond milk, or hemp milk may be used in place of soymilk.

Date Nut Bread
1 8"x4" loaf

This bread is dense and dark-colored and very sweet using only honey and dates as sweeteners. Enjoy the bread sliced as a snack, plain or with a thin spread of almond butter. *Do not slice before fully cooled.* It is good at room temperature the next day but keep it refrigerated after that. If you are not going to use it in a couple of days, freeze half (pre-sliced).

1 cup chopped dates
1 cup boiling water
2 eggs
½ cup honey
¼ cup canola oil
1 tsp vanilla extract
Grated zest of a whole orange
2 ¼ cups gluten-free flour mix
2 tsp xanthan gum
2 tsp aluminum-free baking powder
1 cup chopped pecans

Preheat oven to 350°.
Lightly oil an 8"x4" loaf pan.
Place dates in a medium bowl, pour 1 cup boiling water over them, and allow them to sit for 15 minutes.
Meanwhile, beat eggs with mixer, add honey and oil and mix together.
Add vanilla, orange zest, xanthan gum, baking powder, and gluten-free flour mix and mix with beaters.
Remove beaters and stir in the dates and pecans until fully combined and no dry ingredients remain.
Pour the batter into the prepared pan.
Bake for 1 to 1¼ hours until lightly browned and a toothpick inserted into center comes out clean.
Let bread cool in pan for 10 minutes.
Run knife around the edge and invert the bread onto a cooling rack or clean kitchen towel.

Allow to fully cool before attempting to slice; the bread will be more solid and less apt to crumble.

Use a serrated bread knife to slice this bread and if needed, turn the bread over and slice from the bottom to prevent crumbling.

Greek Lentil Olive Spread
Makes about 2¾ cups

This spread disappeared within 24 hours the first time I made it. The Nori seaweed is a substitute for the anchovies in the original recipe. Serve the spread with rice crackers, *Easy Greek Salad*, and the *Rice Chard Pilaf* for a Greek style dinner.

1 cup lentils, rinsed
2½ cups water
¼ cup Kalamata black olives
2 Tbsp capers, drained and rinsed
½ sheet Nori seaweed, snipped into small pieces
2 Tbsp dried oregano
2 medium cloves garlic
¼ cup fresh lemon juice
2 Tbsp extra virgin olive oil
Sea salt to taste
Fresh parsley, finely chopped

Rinse lentils and place in saucepan with water.
Bring to a boil, turn down heat to simmer and cook for about 30 minutes or until lentils are tender but still hold their shape. Drain and cool.
Place cooled lentils, olives, capers, Nori, oregano and garlic in food processor fitted with steel blade.
Process until well mixed.
Add lemon juice and olive oil and process until blended and fairly smooth.
Sprinkle with fresh parsley and serve with rice crackers or sliced vegetables.

Fig Bars
Makes 20 bars

Many people know that figs are full of iron (3 mg per 5 small figs), but did you know that the average serving size of 5 medium figs packs 126 mg calcium? They are also a great source of fiber, providing about 1 gram of fiber per small fig (and who eats only one?). A real powerhouse fruit!

These bars taste something like those commercially packaged fig bars we all grew up with, but with a healthy fat and only honey and figs for sweetness. Vegans can substitute maple syrup or agave nectar for the honey, and replace the ghee with canola oil or melted Earth Balance trans-fat free margarine.

1¼ cups gluten-free flour mix
¼ cup almond flour
¾ tsp baking soda
1 tsp xanthan gum
¼ tsp sea salt

1½ cups dried Mission figs (the dark ones)
1 Tbsp ghee, melted
3 Tbsp canola oil
¼ cup honey
¼ cup plain soymilk
1 tsp vanilla

Preheat oven to 350°.
Oil an 8x8 inch baking pan.
Place the figs in a small saucepan and add enough water to cover them.
Bring the water and figs to a boil and then turn off heat and allow to sit for 7 minutes or until soft.
Save the soaking water.
Melt the ghee. In a small bowl combine the melted ghee, canola oil, honey, soymilk and vanilla.
In a medium bowl combine the gluten-free flour mix, almond flour, baking soda, and sea salt.
Add the wet ingredients to the dry and stir to combine.

Remove the soaked figs from the water and place in bowl of food processor.

Add 3-4 Tbsp of the soaking water and process until thick but spreadable.

Place enough of the dough in the baking pan to form a crust (about 2/3), and reserve the rest for the topping.

Press the dough down with your fingers, making sure there are no holes in the crust. It will be between $\frac{1}{4}$-$\frac{1}{2}$ inch thick.

Spread the fig puree evenly over the bottom crust.

Mom's Fruit Compote

When I was growing up, my mom often made stewed prunes in the winter or stewed fresh plums in the summer. The dried fruits are very sweet without any added sugar; I add the pears to cut the sweetness a little. The compote is delicious as a dessert or mixed into hot rice cereal for breakfast. You can also use it as a sauce for pancakes or waffles.

2 cups mixed dried fruits, cut into 1 inch pieces (I like the combination of prunes, peaches, nectarines, apricots, and pears)
2 cups water
1 cinnamon stick
$\frac{1}{4}$ fresh lemon
5 whole cloves
2 whole allspice (ok to omit if you don't have this)
1 16 oz can sliced pears, packed in water or juice

Combine dried fruit, water, cinnamon stick, cloves, allspice and $\frac{1}{4}$ lemon in small saucepan over medium heat.

Bring to a simmer. Simmer over medium low heat for about 30 minutes. The fruit should retain its shape but be tender.

Transfer fruit to a serving bowl or container.

Drain the juice from the canned pears and add these to the fruit compote, tossing to combine.

Cool to warm before serving.

Honey Sweetened Popcorn & Peanuts

This is very simple to make and can be packaged in festive food bags for a great holiday gift that is tasty and not full of processed ingredients. The ghee adds a buttery taste but if you want to make it vegan you can use oil and substitute brown rice syrup or agave nectar for the honey. It reminds me of Cracker Jack but a lighter and healthier version.

2 Tbsp ghee
3 Tbsp honey
6-7 cups popped corn kernels, not microwave*
½ cup peanuts, with or without salt
1 Tbsp ground flax

Preheat oven to 350°. You will need a baking pan with a lip.
Line the pan with aluminum foil and lightly oil the foil.
Combine the popcorn and peanuts and spread this evenly in one layer over the foil.
Melt the ghee and honey together over a low heat.
Pour the honey-ghee over the peanut-popcorn and mix with your hands.
Sprinkle the flax over the peanut-popcorn mixture.
Bake for about 20-25 minutes.
It may not seem crisp when you take it out of the oven but it crisps as it cools.
Allow to fully cool and then keep in a sealed container.

*To pop corn kernels in a saucepan, heat a small amount (2 tsp) of canola oil in the saucepan over medium heat. There should be enough oil to cover the bottom of the pot lightly. Pour in enough kernels to cover the bottom, with a little bit of space in between the kernels. Cover the pot. In a short while you will hear the kernels sizzling and they will start to pop. When they begin to pop in earnest, turn the heat to low and, holding the cover on, shake the pan lightly, back and forth to distribute the steam and allow room for the kernels to expand.
The popcorn is done when you no longer hear any kernels popping. Immediately remove from heat or it will burn.

Banana Chocolate Chip Minis
Makes about 32 mini muffins

These egg-free gems are perfect for a child's birthday in school, an after school treat, or an adult indulgence.

Dry ingredients
¾ cup garbanzo (chickpea) flour
¼ cup potato starch
¼ cup tapioca starch
2 tsp baking powder
¼ tsp baking soda
½ tsp xanthan gum
½ tsp sea salt

Wet ingredients
¾ cup mashed banana (about 2 medium)
6 Tbsp agave nectar
6 Tbsp canola oil
2 tsp vanilla extract
¼ tsp almond extract
¾ cup gluten-free dairy-free chocolate chips

Preheat oven to 325°. Lightly oil a mini muffin tin.
Mix together all dry ingredients in a medium sized bowl.
Mix together the wet ingredients in a small bowl.
Add the wet ingredients to the dry and stir to combine.
Stir in the ¾ cup of chocolate chips.
Scoop 1 Tablespoon of the batter into each muffin cup.
You may have to bake these in two batches depending on how many muffins your tin will make or whether you have more than one mini muffin tin.

Bake the minis for 15-18 minutes.
They should be lightly browned and firm on top.
You may also test doneness with a toothpick inserted into the center of a muffin.
When done, remove from oven and ***cool in pan***.
If you remove them too early, they will fall apart.

Melissa's Marvelous Granola

We've been making our own granola for many years but had stopped because gluten-free oats were not readily available at the time. Recently, there are more brands of gluten-free oats available which makes the price more reasonable. Some people with Celiac Disease still do not tolerate oats even though they are certified gluten-free; if you are reintroducing oats to your diet, you may want to proceed gradually.

<u>Dry ingredients</u>
3 cups gluten-free oats
1 cup sliced almonds
1 cup unsweetened shredded coconut (Let's Do Organic has coconut flakes which we love)

<u>Wet ingredients</u>
$\frac{1}{4}$ cup canola oil
$\frac{1}{4}$ cup honey
1 Tbsp vanilla extract

Preheat oven to 350°.
In a large roasting pan, mix dry ingredients together.
Stir together the wet ingredients, then pour over the oats.
Mix everything well to distribute the honey and oil mixture.
Bake for 30 minutes, stirring every 10 minutes, until golden brown.

<u>Variations</u>
Add 2 tsp ground cinnamon with the dry ingredients.
Omit coconut and replace with $\frac{1}{2}$ cup oats and $\frac{1}{2}$ cup raw sunflower seeds.
Use 1 Tbsp maple extract instead of the vanilla.
Replace almonds with walnuts, pecans, or hazelnuts.
Add raisins, dried cranberries or other small pieces of dried fruit after the granola is cooked.

Artichoke Olive Dip
Makes about 1½ cups

My father made this artichoke dip for our first gluten-free Thanksgiving and we all "gobbled" it down. It can also be used as a sandwich spread with roasted red pepper, lettuce and tomato. Or serve stuffed in Belgian endive leaves, or with sliced red pepper or other scoop-like raw vegetables.

1 14-oz can whole artichoke hearts, rinsed well, drained and patted dry
¼ cup olive oil
1 large garlic clove, minced and mashed to a paste with ¼ tsp salt
½ cup brine-cured green olives, pitted and chopped
3 Tb finely chopped parsley leaves

In a food processor, puree artichoke hearts with oil until very smooth, (about 2 minutes).
Transfer puree to a bowl and stir in garlic paste, olives and salt and pepper to taste.
Chill dip covered at least 4 hours and up to 24 hours.
Stir chopped parsley into dip.

My Favorite Shake

This shake is delicious and chocolatey, with the only sweetness derived from frozen very ripe bananas.

1 frozen banana*
1 cup lite vanilla soy milk or rice milk
½ tsp vanilla extract
1 Tbsp unsweetened cocoa powder or carob powder
1 Tbsp maple syrup or agave nectar if needed for sweetness
(or a light sprinkle of stevia powder)

Break up the frozen banana into about four pieces and place in the blender. Add the rest of the ingredients.
Blend until smooth.

* ½ cup frozen strawberries can replace the banana. You may need 1 Tbsp maple syrup or Agave nectar for sweetening as frozen strawberries will have less natural sweetness than the banana.

NOTE: freeze whole, peeled bananas when they become too ripe for enjoyment. Freeze in zipper-close bags for easy retrieval.

Peanut Butter Cereal Bars
20 bars

These cereal bars work with any kind of gluten-free cereal. I've even added the rice cake crumbs from the bottom of the bag! I prefer a mix of cereals for a varied taste and texture. The cereal bars can be wrapped individually in waxed paper for a take-along breakfast or snack. Feel free to substitute almond or any other nut butter.

1 cup natural, unsweetened peanut butter, creamy or chunky*
½ cup gluten-free brown rice syrup, agave nectar, or honey (or more, to taste)
¼ cup canola oil
3 cups gluten-free puffed millet, puffed rice, and/or gluten-free crispy rice cereal (I especially like to add some Perky's Nutty Flax cereal which is very crunchy)
½ cup raisins, or fruit-juice-sweetened dried cranberries or blueberries, chopped apricots, or a mix of all four
¼ cup raw sunflower seeds
2 Tbsp flax seeds

Mix together the peanut butter, brown rice syrup and canola oil.
Place cereal and dried fruits and seeds in a large bowl.
Add the peanut butter mixture and stir until well combined.
Press mixture into a greased 9 x 13 inch baking dish.
Refrigerate, covered, until hard.
Cut into bars, any size. I generally cut them into 20 reasonably sized bars.
Wrap in waxed paper and store in a tightly covered container in the refrigerator. They keep for a long time.

Peanut Butter Chocolate Chip Energy Bars
Makes 16-20 bars depending on how you cut them

Try these variations on the bars: add sliced almonds, add chopped fruit-sweetened dried cherries, or other nuts and fruits, and almond butter or cashew butter may be substituted for the peanut butter. Once cooled, the bars freeze very well.

$1\frac{3}{4}$ cup gluten-free oats (or you can use quinoa flakes)
1 cup gluten-free, dairy-free protein powder
$\frac{1}{2}$ cup gluten-free flour mix
$\frac{1}{2}$ cup almond meal
$\frac{1}{4}$ cup ground flax
1 tsp ground cinnamon
$\frac{1}{2}$ tsp sea salt (this enhances the sweetness)
1 cup gluten-free dairy-free chocolate chips
$\frac{1}{4}$ cup raw sunflower seeds

Wet ingredients
6 Tbsp agave nectar
$\frac{1}{4}$ cup gluten free brown rice syrup
1/3 cup peanut butter
1 Tbsp vanilla extract
1 cup mashed silken tofu

Preheat oven to 350°.
In a large bowl, mix all dry ingredients together.
In a separate bowl, mix the wet ingredients together, mashing the tofu as you mix.
Add the wet ingredients to the dry and mix until uniformly distributed.
Press the mixture into a 9" x 13" baking dish which has been lightly oiled.
Bake the bars for 20 minutes at 350°. Remove them from the oven and cut into the number of bars you want.
Place the cut bars on a lightly oiled baking sheet and bake a second time for 5-8 minutes until lightly browned.
Let the bars cool completely before eating.

"Raw" Chocolate Fudge

This simple recipe can be made in minutes (if you have date paste already prepared) and then refrigerated for a couple of hours for best results. Raw cacao nibs cost $10 per half pound but I must say that using the nibs (ground in a spice grinder) really adds something to the results. A tiny piece of this fudge goes a long way to providing a very satisfying sweet taste without boosting your craving for refined sugar sweets.

$\frac{1}{4}$ cup date paste*
$\frac{1}{4}$ cup raw almond butter
1 Tbsp agave nectar
$\frac{1}{4}$ cup cocoa or carob powder or ground raw cacao nibs (yum!)
1 Tbsp ground flax

Mix everything together and spread in a square container, about 5" x 5". Refrigerate for 2 hours before eating some. The consistency of almond butter and homemade date paste can vary, some will be more liquid and some drier, so you may need to increase the dry ingredients (ground flax and cocoa powder) a bit. Or you can add some chopped nuts to the "batter" for extra crunch.

Variation: add shredded unsweetened coconut or raw, dried shredded unsweetened coconut (the prepackaged kind).

*date paste
In a small saucepan place $\frac{1}{2}$ cup pitted dates. Add water to cover. Bring to a boil, turn down heat and simmer on low for 5 minutes. Cover the pan and turn off heat.
Set aside until cooled; they will continue to steam and soften. Once cooled, puree the dates with whatever is left of the liquid. This is your date paste.

Peanut Butter Chocolate Crunch
Makes about 17

The combination of peanut butter and chocolate is one of my favorites!!! These are also crispy! I guarantee the SECOND time you make them, you will double this recipe. All I have to say is YUM!

¼ cup natural unsweetened peanut butter
2 Tbsp agave nectar
2 Tbsp gluten-free brown rice syrup
1 ½ cups gluten free crispy rice cereal (not flakes, use a Rice Krispies-type)
1 Tbsp cocoa powder

In a small saucepan over low heat melt together the peanut butter, brown rice syrup, and maple syrup, stirring constantly until combined and smooth.
Remove from heat and stir in cocoa powder. Stir until smooth.
Add the rice cereal and stir lightly until the cereal is coated.
Make tablespoon-size balls and place 1 inch apart on waxed paper lined plate (you will need two).
Refrigerate until firm.
Try to keep some for yourself before serving to other household members....or you won't get any.

Popped Sorghum

I've worked with several clients who had food sensitivity to corn which ruled out quite a few gluten-free options; many gluten-free mixes have corn flour or another form of corn. I discovered that popping whole sorghum grain tastes remarkably like popped corn! It is made the same old fashioned way as corn kernels popped in a saucepan with some oil.

Whole grain sorghum
Canola or olive oil
Sea salt

In a saucepan of any size with a tight-fitting lid, over medium heat, warm enough oil to just cover the bottom of the pan. Add enough sorghum to barely cover the bottom of the pan and cover the pot with the lid.

Once you hear the first kernels popping, shake the pan horizontally while holding the lid in place.

Continue to cook this way over medium heat until no more kernels are popping.

Transfer popped sorghum to a bowl and sprinkle with sea salt to taste.

Tofu Eggless Salad

Tofu eggless salad is a pretty close substitute for egg salad. Try it on toasted gluten-free bread with lettuce, tomato and Vegenaise. Add some crispy lightly fried dulse seaweed or a slice or two of tempeh bacon (see Main Dishes).

$\frac{1}{2}$ lb firm or extra firm tofu
2 tsp gluten-free mayo or Vegenaise (a no-egg, vegan mayo)
$\frac{1}{2}$ tsp canola oil
1 tsp cider vinegar
1/8 tsp sea salt
$\frac{1}{4}$ cup thinly sliced scallions
$\frac{1}{4}$ cup thinly sliced celery
$\frac{1}{2}$ tsp dried dill
$\frac{1}{2}$ tsp turmeric
1/8 tsp celery seed

In a small bowl mash tofu until it is the consistency of egg salad.
Add remaining ingredients and mix until combined.
Add more sea salt and mayo, if needed, to taste.
Serve with rice crackers or on slices of cucumber.

Zoe's Snacks
Makes 8-10

Our cousin Sharyl Hoepfinger is raising her children without refined sugar and she sent this simple recipe with many combinations. They remind us of a food bar that is on the market these days for lots of money.

¼ cup of nuts or seeds
1-1½ cups pitted raw dates or other dried fruits, alone or in combination

In a food processor fitted with a steel blade, process nuts or seeds until they resemble coarse crumbs. Add fruit, then process until fairly smooth and sticky (this may take a while depending on how dry the dates are, so be patient). Remove the sticky "dough" and roll into 1" balls (or any creative shape you like). If you like, you can roll any of these in unsweetened coconut or toasted unsweetened coconut. Store the snacks in a tightly sealed container.

<u>Variation</u> For a thicker, stiffer consistency, use ½ cup nuts or seeds with 1 cup of dates and dried fruit.

Try these combinations
<u>Cranberry-almond</u>
¼ cup almonds, ½ cup dates, ½ cup fruit juice sweetened cranberries

<u>Brownie bites</u>
¼ cup walnuts, 1 cup dates, 2 Tbsp unsweetened cocoa Powder, and 1 tsp vanilla extract

<u>Sunflower-apricot</u>
¼ cup sunflower seeds, ½ cup dates, ½ cup dried apricots

Cherry-almond
½ cup cherries, ½ cup dates, ¼ cup almonds, ¼ tsp almond extract

Blueberry-pecan
¼ cup pecans, ¼ cup raisins, ¼ cup dates, 1 cup unsweetened dried blueberries with a bit of cinnamon

Cherry-chocolate
¼ cup almonds, ½ cup dates, ½ cup dried cherries, and 2 Tbsp unsweetened cocoa powder

Cranberry-orange
½ cup dates, ½ cup dried cranberries, ¼ cup almonds and grated orange rind of 1 orange

Gingerbread
1 cup dates, ¼ cup almonds, 1 tsp ground ginger, ¼ tsp ground cinnamon

Cinnamon Stick
1 cup dates, ½ cup pecans, 1¼ tsp ground cinnamon, ½ tsp vanilla extract

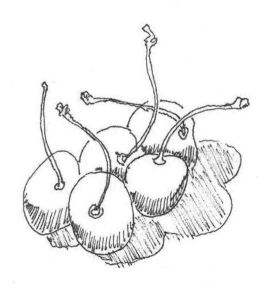

White Bean Spread

This is a low fat spread made from white beans and garlic, with very little oil. White beans have a very pleasant, mild flavor that easily absorbs other flavors added to them. This is a nice alternative to hummus which contains sesame, to which some people are allergic. The bean spread can be used on crackers, salads, sandwiches, or with raw veggies.

14-16 oz. can small white beans (cannellini beans), drained and rinsed
1 clove garlic
2 tsp olive oil
1 tsp fresh lemon juice
1-2 tsp chopped fresh rosemary (if fresh rosemary is not available, you may substitute dried)
Sea salt and freshly ground black pepper to taste

In a food processor fitted with the metal blade, finely mince the garlic.
Add the beans and process.
Add the olive oil, lemon juice, and rosemary, and process.
Add water 1 Tbsp at a time until desired consistency is reached.
Season with sea salt and pepper.

<u>Add-ins</u>
$\frac{1}{4}$ cup chopped roasted red pepper
Fresh basil or parsley
Chopped Kalamata olives

Desserts

Gluten Free / Casein Free Baking Ingredients

<u>Gluten Free Flours</u>
Amaranth flour
Buckwheat flour
Brown rice flour, Superfine by Authentic Foods
Coconut flour, strong coconut flavor
Corn flour
Garbanzo flour, good texture, has a bean taste
Garfava flour, good texture, has a bean taste
Millet flour
Nut flours — Almond meal, Pecan meal, Hazelnut meal
Potato starch flour
Quinoa flour
Sorghum flour, Superfine by Authentic Foods
Soy flour, has a strong taste
Sweet rice flour, Authentic Foods
Tapioca starch flour
Teff flour
White rice flour, Superfine by Authentic Foods

<u>Unrefined Gluten Free Sweeteners</u>
Date sugar
Maple sugar
Gluten-free brown rice syrup
100% pure maple syrup
Honey (local)
Date puree - Cook dried dates in water to cover until soft
          enough to mash. Puree. Store refrigerated. Can also
          use raisins or prunes but they have a stronger flavor.
Wax Orchards fruit juice concentrate
Agave nectar
Apple juice
Applesauce, unsweetened
Banana, mashed

Desserts

Egg Replacers
EnerG brand egg replacer
      mix 1½ tsp with 2 Tbsp warm water to make substitute
      for one egg
      only use as substitute in baked goods, works as
      leavening agent, not as binder
Flax meal
      1 Tbsp ground flax plus 3 Tbsp water, blend for 1 -2
      min and let sit for 2-3 min until consistency of egg is
      reached. Will not help with rising, makes foods chewier
Silken tofu
      ¼ cup, blended until smooth, provides the binder but
      not the leavening
Applesauce and mashed banana can both be used as binders
but not as leavening agents

Milk Substitutes
Almond milk
Rice milk
Soy milk
Coconut milk
Buttermilk substitute
      Combine 2 Tbsp cider vinegar with 1 cup plain soy milk
      to get a substitute that will work in recipes calling for
      buttermilk
Hemp milk —   Hemp Bliss, Living Naturals

Dairy Free Solid Shortenings
Spectrum brand trans fat-free, gluten-free, casein-free
shortening
Willow Run dairy-free soy margarine
Coconut oil
Purity Farms ghee (clarified butter which is gluten-free,
lactose-free, and casein- free)
Earth Balance trans fat-free, gluten-free, casein-free, vegan
tub margarine
Earth Balance trans fat-free, gluten-free, casein-free, vegan
margarine sticks

Gluten Free Dairy Free Chocolate

There are several brands of dairy-free and sugar-free chocolate chips, however, some are grain-sweetened with malted barley and these are not gluten-free. Look for chips that contain only sugar, chocolate liquor, non-dairy cocoa butter, and soy lecithin. Goodbaker.com has vegan chocolate chips. If you are highly sensitive to trace amounts of gluten and dairy you will want to check with the chocolate chip company to make sure the vanilla is gluten-free. Or just stick with brands that are labeled gluten- and dairy-free.

Enjoy Life semi-sweet chocolate chips
> Enjoy Life brand of chocolate chips is dairy-free and made in a dedicated gluten-free, nut-free facility.

Tropical Source semi-sweet chocolate chips
Rapunzel semi-sweet chocolate chips
Natural unsweetened cocoa powder
Wax Orchards *Oh, Fudge!*, fat-free, fruit-sweetened chocolate fudge
> Ingredients: unsweetened pineapple syrup, pear juice concentrate, Dutch cocoa, natural flavor. 1 Tbsp has 45 calories, 0 grams fat.

Leavening Agents

Aluminum-free baking powder
Baking soda

Corn-free baking powder recipe

Combine:
> $1\frac{1}{4}$ Tbsp baking soda
>
> $2\frac{1}{2}$ Tbsp cream of tartar
>
> $2\frac{1}{2}$ Tbsp arrowroot powder or tapioca starch

Stir well with wire whisk and store in a glass jar.

Gluten Free Baking Tips

<u>Gluten-free flour mixes</u>
I keep two different gluten-free flour mixes on hand all the time and I keep a label inside the jar with the recipe. This way it is easy to replenish my supply without having to take out a cookbook, and I always know which flour mix is which.

Why use a gluten-free flour mix instead of just a single gluten-free flour? The rice flour and other gluten-free flours tend to be a little gritty but mixing the rice flour with tapioca starch and potato starch "lightens" the flour, making the texture closer to wheat flour. Gluten-free flour mix can be used to replace regular flour in any recipe.

Gluten-free flour has less protein than wheat flour. In fact, wheat gluten is the protein in wheat flour and provides the elasticity in baking. Successful gluten-free baking requires more ingredients that provide protein to the recipe such as eggs, and milk. Many gluten-free recipes add plain gelatin for additional protein. Since gelatin is an animal product, it is not used in any of my recipes; however, you may see more eggs, soymilk and tofu.

Another important ingredient of gluten-free baking is xanthan gum. Xanthan gum comes from the fermentation of corn sugar, although there is no corn residue in the end result. Xanthan gum helps to prevent crumbling and is used in small amounts, about 1 tsp per cup of gluten-free flour in a recipe.

Lastly, gluten-free flours may require some extra help with rising. These recipes may contain more baking powder, more baking soda, or more eggs to get the volume that we are used to with wheat flour baking.

Note: *all my recipes have been created using a convection oven. Your baking times may change slightly.*

An important tip: when using a gluten-free flour mix, do not dip your measuring cup into the container to scoop out the flour. Rather, spoon out the flour into the measuring cup. This helps with "lightening" the gluten-free flour.

Rice Flour Mix
Makes 5 cups

4 cups rice flour (I like the texture of superfine white rice or superfine brown rice flour from Authentic Foods)
1 cup potato starch
1 cup tapioca flour

Sorghum-millet Flour Mix
Makes 5 cups

1 cup sorghum flour (Authentic Foods has a superfine sorghum flour)
$1\frac{1}{2}$ cup tapioca flour (tapioca starch)
$1\frac{1}{2}$ cup potato starch (not potato flour)
1 cup millet flour (or corn flour)

In a dry sifter, place all ingredients for the flour mix.
Sift mixture into a large bowl.
Spoon flour mix back into sifter and sift again.
Sift a third time.
Give the mix a final stir with a wire whisk and then spoon it into a wide-mouth jar or container with an air-tight lid.

Apple Date Nut Bars
Makes 36 bars

I love the combination of flavors in these bars. The base and topping are slightly sweet and rich tasting, with a pecan-cinnamon overtone like a coffee cake, while the dates and apples are very sweet and provide a contrasting texture to the "crumble".

The recipe makes quite a few bars but they freeze well; unless you're serving a crowd I would suggest freezing half.

2 large apples, peeled and chopped finely
2 Tbsp Wax Orchards Fruit Sweet concentrated fruit juice blend* or agave nectar
2 Tbsp lemon juice
2 Tbsp water
1½ cups dates, chopped
3 Tbsp casein-free ghee or Earth Balance non-hydrogenated vegan margarine
¼ cup canola oil
2 Tbsp brown rice syrup
2 Tbsp maple syrup
¼ tsp salt
2½ cups gluten-free flour mix
1½ cups chopped pecans
1½ tsp ground cinnamon

In a small saucepan, combine apples, fruit juice concentrate, lemon juice and water.
Simmer covered for 5-10 minutes until tender.
Add dates and continue simmering, uncovered, for about 5 minutes, mashing the dates with a fork, until the dates are soft and the mixture is almost smooth. Let cool.
Combine ghee, canola oil, brown rice syrup, maple syrup, salt, gluten-free flour mix, pecans, and cinnamon in a bowl and blend well.
The mixture will be crumbly with some of it holding together.
Press ½ of the flour mixture into a 9"x13" baking dish. Spread the date-apple puree evenly over the flour base.

Crumble the rest of the flour mixture over the puree.
Bake the bars at 375° for 35-40 minutes until lightly browned.
Cool completely before cutting into bars.
If storing for more than a day or two, they will need to be
kept in the refrigerator in a tin or airtight container.

*honey or agave nectar may be substituted

Pears Poached in Wine
Makes 4 pears, easily multiplied

I don't usually like Bartlett pears for eating because they tend
to be more "mealy" than Anjou or Red pears, but they are
great for poaching as they have that classic curvy pear shape
which looks beautiful when wine-tinged. If you are not allowed
to have wine, you can use cider, apple, or orange juice for the
poaching and reduce the sweetener by half since the juices are
already sweet. If poaching in juice, add a tsp of vanilla extract
to the "reduced" sauce before serving over the pears.

4 Anjou pears, firm but ripe
1 bottle of red wine
1 3-inch piece of orange peel
1 cinnamon stick
$\frac{1}{4}$ cup maple syrup
$\frac{1}{4}$ cup brown rice syrup
Peel, halve, and core the pears.
In a large heavy saucepan bring the wine, orange peel, cinnamon
stick, maple syrup and brown rice syrup to a simmer.

Add the pears, and simmer covered, turning occasionally, 10-15
min until tender.
Remove pears to bowls.
Boil poaching syrup until there is about $\frac{3}{4}$ cup.
Cool and pour over pears.
Serve chilled or warm.

Almond Espresso Chocolate Chip Cookies
Makes about 18 cookies

The combination of almonds, chocolate, and espresso is unbelievable, and the nuts give these a great crunchy texture. They freeze well, so make a batch and freeze half for another time.

1¼ cup coarsely chopped whole almonds, this is best done by hand to get the right texture)
1½ cup gluten-free flour mix
1 Tbsp espresso powder
¼ cup cocoa powder
½ tsp xanthan gum
1/8 tsp sea salt
5 Tbsp pure maple syrup
¼ cup gluten-free brown rice syrup
2 Tbsp agave nectar
5 Tbsp canola oil
½ tsp vanilla extract
½ cup gluten-free, dairy-free chocolate chips

Place chopped nuts, gluten-free flour mix, espresso powder, cocoa powder, and xanthan gum in a large bowl.
In a smaller bowl combine maple syrup, brown rice syrup, agave nectar, canola oil, and vanilla.
Add the wet ingredients to the dry and mix until combined.
The dough will be very stiff and sticky.
Add the chocolate chips and mix in.
Preheat oven to 350°.
On a lightly oiled baking sheet place large globs of dough (about a heaping tablespoon each) and shape by making them somewhat round and flattening the globs to ¼-inch thick with your fingers or a fork. Works best with 9 cookies per baking sheet.
Bake for about 15 minutes.
Cool on the baking sheet for 5 minutes before removing to a cooling rack.

Cinnamon Pecan Coffee Cake

With this recipe I was trying to come close to the bakery crumb buns that my mother-in-law likes to have on Christmas morning which have an inch of brown sugar crumbs on top of the cake bottom. This coffee cake has a great flavor and is satisfying for a special holiday morning even though the topping is not thick crumbs but more of a sprinkle.

2/3 cup maple syrup
1/3 cup canola oil
1 egg
1/3 cup plain soy milk
2 $\frac{1}{4}$ cups gluten-free flour mix
2 tsp xanthan gum
1 tsp salt
1 Tbsp baking powder

Topping:
$\frac{1}{2}$ cup gluten-free flour mix, 4 Tbsp date sugar and 2 Tbsp maple sugar, $\frac{1}{4}$ cup quinoa flakes, $\frac{1}{2}$ tsp cinnamon, 2 Tbsp ghee (not melted), 1 Tbsp canola oil.

Optional: $\frac{1}{4}$ cup finely chopped pecans, hazelnuts, or walnuts. **It is truly much more delicious with the nuts!**

Preheat oven to 350°. Lightly oil a 9x13 inch baking dish.
In a mixing bowl, mix together the maple syrup, canola oil, egg, and soy milk. Add the xanthan gum, salt, and baking powder and mix to combine.
Gradually add the flour and mix to combine.
Pour batter into prepared baking dish.
Combine topping ingredients using a fork to incorporate the ingredients. The mixture will be crumbly.
Sprinkle the topping over the batter.
Bake for 35-40 minutes until toothpick inserted in the center comes out clean.
Note: Egg replacer can be used. 6 Tbsp sucanat sugar can be used instead of the date and maple sugar.

Completely Delicious Cocoa Brownies
16 brownies, I like to cut them fairly small

I have served these to unsuspecting guests and family members without telling them about all the "weird" ingredients. They are rich, fudge-like, and plenty sweet despite the lack of refined sugar, and the use of the cocoa powder allows me to reduce the fat somewhat. The nuts add more to the texture but you can omit them (but not the almond flour) or try the other variations. These are completely delicious.

2 Tbsp ghee, melted
2 Tbsp canola oil
$\frac{1}{2}$ cup gluten-free brown rice syrup
$\frac{1}{2}$ cup pure maple syrup
2 eggs
$\frac{1}{2}$ cup cocoa powder
$\frac{3}{4}$ cup almond flour (almond meal)
$\frac{3}{4}$ cup gluten-free flour mix
2 tsp vanilla
$\frac{1}{4}$ tsp almond extract (optional but tasty)
$\frac{1}{4}$ cup chopped nuts (sliced almonds or chopped pecans are wonderful)

In a medium sized bowl, stir together the melted ghee, oil, rice syrup and maple syrup.
Add eggs, cocoa powder, almond flour, gluten-free flour mix, and vanilla. Stir until fully combined.
Stir in nuts.
Pour into an 8x8 inch baking pan which has been sprayed with cooking spray or lightly oiled.
Bake 350° F for 25-30 min. until a toothpick inserted into the center comes out clean.
Cool before cutting.

Notes:

Carob powder may be substituted for the cocoa powder.

Canola oil may be substituted for the ghee.

½ cup creamed silken tofu may be substituted for the eggs.

Peanut Butter Swirl Brownies

Follow ingredients and directions as above, omitting the ¼ cup chopped nuts.

Pour the brownie batter into the pan.

Mix together 2/3 cup unsweetened smooth peanut butter, 1 Tbsp canola oil, and 2 Tbsp maple sugar.

Drop the peanut butter mixture in blobs over the chocolate mixture.

With a spreading knife, swirl the peanut butter mixture into the chocolate mixture, creating a marble effect.

Bake as above.

Espresso Brownies

Follow the ingredients and directions as above, omitting the ghee and using ¼ cup canola oil.

Use only 1 tsp vanilla extract.

Add 1½ Tbsp instant espresso powder.

Ginger Molasses Cookies
Makes about 20 cookies

These spicy gingery cookies are egg-free. We were so excited when I first took them out of the oven and "heard" them being placed on the cooling rack. In other words, they were crispy enough to have a sound! These are the first gluten-free cookies that we have had that are crisp, and we are so pleased to share them with you.

1 cup whole almonds

1 cup quinoa flakes

½ cup brown rice flour

¼ cup potato starch

¼ cup tapioca starch

½ tsp xanthan gum

4 tsp ground ginger
1 tsp ground cinnamon
½ tsp mace
½ tsp sea salt
¼ cup pure maple syrup
¼ cup blackstrap molasses
1 tsp vanilla
1/3 cup canola oil

Preheat oven to 325°. Toast the almonds on a cookie sheet for about 10 minutes. Remove from heat and cool. Place almonds in food processor and pulse until they become crumbs.
In a large bowl, combine the quinoa flakes, ground almonds, brown rice flour, potato starch, tapioca starch, xanthan gum, ginger, cinnamon, mace, and sea salt.
Whisk until fully combined.
In a separate bowl combine the maple syrup, molasses, vanilla, and oil.
Add the wet ingredients to the dry and mix well.
Roll balls of the dough, about the size of ½ Tbsp, and place on greased cookie sheet.
Smush the balls slightly with the palm of your hand, then flatten to ¼ inch thick with the back of a fork. It may take about 10 presses with the back of your fork to get to ¼ inch. The cookies will be around 4 inches in diameter. It helps to dip the fork in water occasionally to prevent dough from sticking, making sure to shake the water off the fork before continuing to press out the cookies.
The fork tines make a nice pattern on the cookies.
Bake 20 minutes. Remove from oven and allow to cool on cookie sheet for 5 minutes before removing to a cooling rack.

Granola Cookies
Makes 9

These egg-free cookies are both chewy and crunchy from the combined oats and pumpkin seeds. They are so wholesome I think you could eat one for breakfast!

$\frac{3}{4}$ cup gluten-free oats
2 Tbsp teff flour
2 Tbsp sorghum flour
$\frac{1}{4}$ cup millet flour
$\frac{1}{4}$ cup tapioca starch
1 tsp xanthan gum
$\frac{1}{2}$ cup unsweetened shredded coconut
$\frac{1}{2}$ cup pumpkin seeds (pepitas)
$\frac{1}{2}$ cup raisins
$\frac{1}{2}$ cup chopped dates
$\frac{1}{4}$ tsp nutmeg
$\frac{1}{4}$ tsp allspice
$\frac{1}{2}$ tsp cinnamon
1/3 cup canola oil
$\frac{1}{2}$ cup maple syrup
$\frac{1}{4}$ cup unsweetened applesauce
1 tsp vanilla

Preheat oven to 350°. Lightly oil a baking sheet.
In a medium bowl, combine oats, flours, tapioca starch, xanthan gum, coconut, pumpkin seeds, raisins, dates, and spices.
In a separate bowl combine the oil, maple syrup, applesauce, and vanilla.
Add the wet ingredients to the dry and mix until fully combined.
To form each cookie, fill $\frac{1}{4}$ cup measure with dough and invert onto baking sheet.
Flatten slightly with your fingers to $\frac{1}{2}$ inch thick.
Bake for 18 minutes. Remove from oven. They may look a bit light colored but that is ok.
Leave the cookies on the baking sheet until fully cooled.

Gram's Spice Cookies

My husband's grandmother gave us her recipe for wonderful spice cookies which she rolled and cut into holiday shapes at Christmas time. These cookies are a re-make and though they are not rolled and cut, if we close our eyes they taste just like Gram's.

1 cup whole almonds, toasted 10 minutes at 325°, then finely chopped
1 cup quinoa flakes
$\frac{1}{2}$ cup brown rice flour
$\frac{1}{4}$ cup potato starch
$\frac{1}{4}$ cup tapioca starch
$\frac{1}{2}$ tsp xanthan gum
2 tsp cinnamon
$\frac{1}{2}$ tsp ginger
$1\frac{1}{2}$ tsp cloves
$1\frac{1}{2}$ tsp mace
$\frac{1}{4}$ cup brown rice syrup
$\frac{1}{4}$ cup maple syrup
1/3 cup canola oil
$\frac{1}{2}$ tsp lemon extract
1 tsp vanilla

Preheat oven to 350°.
In a large bowl, combine the quinoa flakes, finely chopped almonds, brown rice flour, potato starch, tapioca starch, xanthan gum, cinnamon, ginger, cloves, and mace.
Whisk until fully combined.
In a separate bowl combine the brown rice syrup, maple syrup, oil, vanilla, and lemon extract.
Add the wet ingredients to the dry and mix well.
Roll balls of the dough, about the size of $\frac{1}{2}$ Tbsp, and place on lightly greased cookie sheet.
Smush the balls slightly with the palm of your hand, then flatten to $\frac{1}{4}$ inch thick with the back of a fork. It may take about 10 presses with the back of your fork to get to $\frac{1}{4}$ inch. The cookies will be around 4 inches in diameter. It helps to dip

the fork in water occasionally to prevent dough from sticking, making sure to shake the water off the fork before continuing to press out the cookies.

The fork tines make a nice pattern on the cookies.

Bake the cookies for 18 minutes.

Remove from oven and cool on pan for 2 minutes, then remove to a cooling rack.

Maple Walnut Baked Apples
Makes 4

My children prefer desserts without raisins so I stuff these apples with nuts instead. The maple syrup does add a bit of sugar, but the result is rich-tasting, sweet, nutty, and satisfying. Serve with a dollop of vanilla flavored soy ice cream (we like Turtle Mountain fruit-sweetened It's Soy Delicious) for an elegant dessert worthy of special guests.

4 firm apples (Golden Delicious, Gala, or Fuji)
1 cup orange juice
$\frac{1}{4}$ cup maple syrup
$\frac{1}{4}$ tsp cinnamon
4 Tbsp chopped walnuts or pecans

Preheat oven to 350°.

Peel a 1-inch wide strip from the top of the apples and remove the cores.

Place the apples in a deep casserole.

Combine the juice, maple syrup, and cinnamon in a glass measuring cup and microwave for 1 minute.

Stir with a wire whisk.

Stuff the apple cavities with chopped walnuts.

Pour the juice over the apples and into the cavities.

Most of the juice will end up in the bottom of the casserole.

Bake the apples at 350° for 1 hour, basting with the juice every 15 minutes.

Serve each person 1 apple with some of the remaining juice spooned over the top.

Pecan Turtle Bars
Makes 18 bars

My mother-in-law used to make these for Valentine's Day and they were so luscious with a buttery crust, gooey caramel, and topped with pecans and melted chocolate. We think this recipe comes pretty close.

Crust
2 cups gluten-free flour mix
3 Tbsp ghee
4 Tbsp Wax Orchards concentrated fruit juice blend

Caramel Layer
2 Tbsp ghee
2 Tbsp soy margarine or coconut oil
2 Tbsp concentrated fruit juice blend
¼ cup gluten-free brown rice syrup

1 cup pecan halves
½ cup dairy-free chocolate chips*

Preheat the oven to 350°.
In a medium sized bowl, combine crust ingredients and blend well with a fork or pastry cutter.
Press this mixture into a 6"x12" baking dish.
In a small saucepan, combine caramel layer ingredients and cook over low heat, stirring continuously until ingredients have blended together.
Place pecan halves over crust. Pour caramel layer over pecans. Bake for about 25 minutes, until caramel layer is bubbly and bottom crust is lightly browned.
Let the bars cool for 5 minutes then sprinkle with chocolate chips.
Let the chips melt undisturbed for 5 minutes, then, using a spreading knife, swirl the melted chocolate over the bars.
Let bars cool completely before cutting. Cut into 18 bars.

Pumpkin Custard
Makes 2 crustless pies
This recipe makes a lot but I have written the amounts for one crustless pie at the end of the recipe. The custard provides plenty of vitamin A and protein so don't feel guilty if you want to eat it for breakfast. Go ahead!

1 29-oz can pumpkin puree (organic if you prefer)
4 large eggs, beaten
1 box silken tofu (12 oz) blended with 1 can coconut milk (14 oz) in blender
1/3 cup honey
2/3 cup maple syrup
2 tsp cinnamon
1 tsp ginger
½ tsp cloves

In a large mixing bowl, combine pumpkin, eggs, tofu-coconut milk mixture, honey, maple syrup, and spices.
Transfer to 2 glass pie dishes or 2 large oiled custard dishes (2 -quart).
For a nicer presentation, pour custard into 6 oz ramekins and bake; they may take less time than the bigger dishes.
Bake 425° for 15 minutes then reduce temperature to 350° for 40-50 minutes or until knife inserted near center comes out clean.

<u>Proportions for one crustless pie</u>
1¾ cups pumpkin puree, 2 eggs, 6 oz silken tofu blended with 6 oz coconut milk, 3 Tbsp honey, 1/3 cup maple syrup, 1 tsp cinnamon, ½ tsp ginger, ¼ tsp cloves

Rosemary Shortbread
Makes 18 small wedges or 8-16 larger wedges

Rosemary is an herb that we are used to seeing in savory recipes like stews and soups. Combined with the buttery ghee and other shortbread ingredients the rosemary takes on a "sweeter" herb taste. These are easy to make but very elegant to serve. I love to make them in mini tartlet pans ($4\frac{1}{2}$ inches across) which gives them a fluted edge. These are great for a Mother's Day luncheon.

3 Tbsp dairy-free margarine and 3 Tbsp ghee (I use Purity Farms which is lactose- and casein-free)
1 Tbsp honey
$\frac{1}{4}$ cup maple sugar
1 cup gluten-free flour mix
$\frac{1}{2}$ tsp aluminum-free baking powder
$\frac{1}{2}$ tsp sea salt
1 tsp xanthan gum
1 Tbsp finely minced fresh rosemary leaves (do not use dried rosemary)

Preheat oven to 350°.
In a mixing bowl, cream soy margarine and ghee with honey and maple sugar until creamy.
In a separate bowl combine gluten-free flour mix, baking powder, salt, xanthan gum, and rosemary.
Add dry ingredients to the creamed margarine mixture and mix until well combined into a dough.

You can either use three $4\frac{1}{2}$-inch tartlet pans with removable bottoms and fluted edges or one 9-inch cake pan, lightly sprayed with canola oil.
For the tartlet pans, divide the dough evenly amongst the three pans and press down evenly with your fingers.
Score the shortbread into 6 wedges per pan by creating dividing marks with the tines a fork dipped in gluten-free flour. Start by making a peace sign and then dividing each of the three sections in two.

For the cake pan, place all the dough in the pan and press down evenly with your fingers. Score the dough into 8 or 16 wedges. If desired, you can decorate the edge with the flat side of the fork.
Bake the shortbread for 25 minutes or until golden.
Remove from oven and let stand for 10 minutes before unmolding.

To unmold the tartlets, turn them over onto a clean kitchen towel and remove sides and bottom.
Turn them onto a cutting board and cut through the shortbread on the score marks. Let wedges cool.

To unmold the cake pan, run a small knife around the edge of the pan and invert onto a kitchen towel.
Turn onto a cutting board and cut through the shortbread on the score marks. Let wedges cool.

Tofu Ricotta Crème with Cherries & Almonds

1 14-16 oz package water-packed extra firm tofu, drained
$\frac{1}{4}$ cup maple syrup (or 3 Tbsp plus a sprinkle of stevia powder)
$\frac{1}{2}$ tsp almond extract
$\frac{1}{2}$ tsp vanilla extract
1 pkg frozen cherries
$\frac{1}{4}$ cup toasted almonds, slices or slivers
Ground cinnamon for sprinkling

In a food processor fitted with the steel blade, process the tofu, syrup, and extracts until smooth. Transfer to a bowl.
Place the fruit in a microwave-proof bowl and heat for 1 minute in the microwave, or until warmed.
In 6 oz ramekins, divide the cherries equally.
Put a dollop of tofu ricotta crème on top of each (about a heaping tablespoon), sprinkle lightly with cinnamon, and top with 1 Tbsp toasted almonds.
Serve.
Any kind of spiced fruit such as sautéed plums will work nicely.

Raspberry Chocolate Cake

This recipe was inspired by one from The Best of Gourmet 2000, which has been my daughter's birthday cake request for several years. It is a small but very rich cake, almost a flourless torte, which is baked "upside down" with its own frosting underneath. Remove the cake by turning it onto a cake plate and the frosting will run down the sides.

½ cup semi-sweet gluten-free, dairy-free chocolate (chips or bar will work)*
½ cup all-fruit raspberry jam, no seeds
½ cup plain soymilk (not lite) or soy creamer
1 Tbsp coconut oil (this is optional but adds some richness)

½ cup **very** hot water
1/3 cup cocoa powder
¼ cup plain soy milk
½ tsp vanilla
1/3 cup all-fruit raspberry jam, no seeds
1/3 cup gluten-free brown rice syrup or maple syrup
¼ cup agave nectar
1/3 cup date sugar
½ cup non-hydrogenated dairy-free margarine (I use Earth Balance)
2 eggs
1 cup gluten-free flour mix
¾ tsp xanthan gum
¾ tsp baking soda
Pinch sea salt

Preheat oven to 350°. Lightly oil a 9-inch round cake pan.
In a small saucepan over medium low heat, melt together the chocolate, ½ cup raspberry jam, ½ cup soymilk, and coconut oil if using, stirring until smooth. Pour this mixture into the cake pan and set aside.
It will start to set while you make the cake batter.

In a small bowl, pour the hot water over the cocoa powder and raspberry jam and stir with a wire whisk until combined.
Add the soy milk and vanilla. Set aside.

In a large mixing bowl combine the margarine, brown rice syrup, maple syrup, and date sugar. Mix until fully combined.
Add the xanthan gum, baking soda, and sea salt. Add eggs and mix well.

Add the cocoa mixture.
Add the gluten-free flour mix and mix until smooth.
Pour this batter over the melted chocolate mixture which is already waiting in the pan.

Bake the cake for about 35 minutes or until a toothpick inserted into the center comes out clean.
(Remember the frosting on the bottom will not be solid!).
Cool the cake for about 10 minutes.
Loosen the cake with a knife and then turn over onto a serving plate and allow the frosting to do what it will.

If you don't plan to serve the cake right away, leave it in the pan and cover with some foil.
Just before serving warm the cake in the oven at 325° for about 5 minutes, or enough to melt the frosting.
Invert the cake and serve.

"Raw" Carrot Cake
Makes 8-12 slices depending on the size

I LOVE carrot cake and have it once a year for my birthday. I have tried many versions of carrot cake and admit that I do like it with the tangy cream cheese frosting. People who like carrot cake are often very specific about what can and cannot be in the cake, such as with or without nuts, pineapple, and coconut. I like mine with all three, the chunkier the better. My "raw" version of carrot cake, full of healthful ingredients, may seem very strange to anyone who has not eaten raw desserts but keep an open mind and I hope you will find it is delicious. Nothing to feel guilty about so I can eat this carrot cake even when it is <u>not</u> my birthday!

2½ cups raw peeled shredded carrots
½ cup pitted dates and ½ cup dried unsulfured pineapple, soaked in water for 1 hour, then drained
¼ cup walnuts
2 Tbsp unsweetened dried coconut
½ cup fresh pineapple
1 tsp vanilla
1 Tbsp coconut oil
1 Tbsp agave nectar
1 tsp cinnamon
¼ tsp each nutmeg and allspice
1/8 tsp each ground cloves and ginger
¼ cup raisins
2 Tbsp dried shredded raw coconut (or more dried coconut if you can't find the raw dried kind)

Frosting:
¾ cup raw cashews, soaked in water overnight
2 Tbsp agave nectar
1 tsp lemon or lime juice
½ tsp vanilla
¼ tsp almond extract
1 Tbsp coconut oil
1-2 Tbsp water

1-2 Tbsp dried shredded raw coconut (optional)

Set aside ½ cup shredded carrot.
Place the remaining 2 cups shredded carrot, soaked dates and pineapple, walnuts, unsweetened coconut, fresh pineapple, vanilla, coconut oil, agave nectar, and spices in the bowl of a food processor with a steel blade. Pulse the mixture until it is coarsely combined but not pulverized and mushy. Transfer the mixture to a bowl and add the ½ cup shredded carrot, the raisins and the dried shredded raw coconut. Mix well.
Transfer the cake batter to an 8-inch springform pan that has been lined with waxed paper, making sure to smooth the batter on the top. Cover with foil and refrigerate at least 1 hour but longer is preferable.

Meanwhile, make the frosting:
Place the cashews, agave nectar, lemon or lime juice, vanilla, and coconut oil in your food processor and process until smooth, adding the water as needed to thin the frosting. It will have the consistency of homemade hummus.
Remove the carrot cake from the refrigerator. Remove the outer ring from the pan and place a cake plate upside down on the carrot cake. Turn the whole thing over so that the cake is on the plate. Peel off the springform bottom and the waxed paper. With your hands, push in the sides of the cake (keeping it round) to shape it. Frost just the top of the cake with the frosting, using it all. Sprinkle the top with the 1-2 Tbsp dried shredded raw coconut.

Refrigerate until serving. Return any leftover cake to the refrigerator.

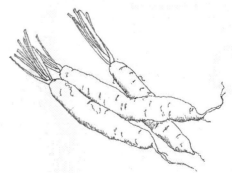

Sautéed Fruit
4 servings

Sautéed fruit tastes like apple pie without the crust. I usually make it when I have too many fruits "turning" such as peaches, nectarines, pears and plums; it works especially well with pears, apples, or ripe peaches. Add ½ cup fresh cranberries to the fall/winter fruits for a beautiful wine color and extra tang; add ½ cup blueberries to the summer fruits for a beautiful purple color.

4 apples or pears (any kind) or a combination, unpeeled, thinly sliced
1 Tbsp ghee or gluten-free casein-free maragarine
1 Tbsp honey or gluten-free brown rice syrup or maple syrup
½ tsp ground cinnamon
¼ tsp ground allspice
Pinch ground nutmeg
Pinch ground cloves
Canola oil cooking spray
Pecans, chopped and toasted lightly (optional)

Spray a nonstick or cast iron pan with the cooking spray or lightly oil the pan with canola oil.
Over medium heat melt the ghee.
Add fruit slices and sweetener.
Turning with a spatula every several seconds, sprinkle with the spices.
Cook about 5-7 minutes until the fruits are warmed and softened but not mushy; there will be a thickened sauce in the pan.

Serve in small bowls as dessert or use to top pancakes and waffles. Sprinkle each portion with 1 Tbsp toasted chopped pecans for an extra treat.

This recipe is easily doubled or tripled; plan on one fruit and 1 tsp ghee per person.

Fall/Winter fruit mix: apples, pears, cranberries, prune plums.

Summer fruit mix: peaches, plums, blueberries, nectarines.

Wilma's Blueberry Torte
8 wedges

One of the things that I really like about this torte is the cup of fresh blueberries that are added on top *after* the torte is baked. Blueberries are loaded with antioxidants and each slice has 1/3 cup of blueberries!

1 cup plus 2 Tbsp gluten-free flour mix
Pinch salt
½ cup + 2 Tbsp date sugar or maple sugar
½ c. casein-free soy margarine or ghee, or half margarine and half ghee* (very cold)
1 Tbsp white vinegar
Dash cinnamon
3 cups fresh blueberries, washed and dried

Combine 1 cup flour, salt, and 2 Tbsp date sugar.
Add margarine or ghee and using a pastry cutter work into flour until it forms crumbs.
Add vinegar for moistening.
Using a 9-inch pan with a loose bottom, spread crust on bottom, about ½ inch up the sides and ¼ inch thick on the bottom.
Make sure there are no holes.
Combine ½ cup date sugar, 2 Tbsp flour, and cinnamon. Add 2 cups blueberries. Sprinkle this mixture over crust.
Bake 400° 45 min. Remove from oven and sprinkle with 1 cup uncooked blueberries. Let cool and remove from pan.

*coconut oil or Spectrum Organic Shortening (palm oil) can be used in place of the soy margarine but must be cold

Seven Fruit Crisps

Rhubarb and cranberries have no natural sugar which is why those recipes have more sugar. Any of the following sweeteners may be used in place of what I have listed: concentrated fruit juice, honey, pure maple syrup, brown rice syrup, agavé nectar. Soy margarine may be used to replace the ghee.

Fruit
Use any of the following combinations:

Cranberry-Apple: 2 cups cranberries (1 12oz pkg), 4 large apples, peeled, cored, and sliced thin, $\frac{1}{2}$ cup honey or maple syrup, 1 tsp cinnamon, 1 Tbsp gluten-free flour. Instead of 4 apples, you can use 2 apples and 2 pears along with the cranberries.

Pear: 5 cups thinly sliced, peeled, cored pears, 1 tsp grated lemon rind, 1 Tbsp lemon juice, 2 Tbsp honey or maple syrup, $\frac{1}{4}$ tsp cinnamon, pinch allspice.

Rhubarb: 5 cups (about $1\frac{1}{2}$ lbs) rhubarb cut into $\frac{1}{2}$-inch slices, 1 tsp grated lemon rind, $\frac{1}{2}$ cup honey or maple syrup.

Peach: Five or six large ripe peaches (about 5 cups), unpeeled and sliced, 1 Tbsp lemon juice, $\frac{1}{4}$ tsp cinnamon, pinch nutmeg, pinch cloves.

Apple: Five or six large apples (about 5 cups), peeled and sliced, 1- 2 Tbsp concentrated fruit juice like Wax Orchard, $\frac{1}{4}$ tsp cinnamon, 1 Tbsp lemon juice, pinch nutmeg, pinch cloves.

Apple Pear: 5 cups peeled and sliced pears and apples, in whatever proportion you wish, 1 Tbsp lemon juice, 1-2 Tbsp concentrated fruit juice, $\frac{1}{4}$ tsp cinnamon, pinch allspice.

<u>Pear Cranberry Ginger</u>: 4 cups peeled and sliced pears, 1 cup fresh cranberries, 1 Tbsp fresh minced ginger, 3 Tbsp honey, 1 Tbsp lemon juice, $\frac{1}{4}$ tsp ground cardamom.

<u>Topping</u>:
$\frac{1}{2}$ cup gluten-free flour mix, 5 Tbsp date or maple sugar, $\frac{1}{4}$ cup quinoa flakes (or gluten-free oats), $\frac{1}{2}$ tsp cinnamon, 2 Tbsp ghee (not melted), 1 Tbsp canola oil.

<u>Optional</u> (but much better with them):
$\frac{1}{4}$ cup finely chopped pecans, hazelnuts, or walnuts.

Preheat oven to 350°.
Oil a 6 cup **_shallow_** baking pan with non-stick cooking spray or canola oil.
Use any of the fruit combinations.
Mix the fruit ingredients in a large bowl.
Spread in pan.
For topping, combine gluten-free flour mix, date sugar, quinoa flakes, and cinnamon in a small bowl.
With pastry blender or a fork blend the ghee or margarine and oil into the dry ingredients until crumbly.
You may want to rub the mixture between your fingertips to get the crumb effect.
If you are adding chopped nuts, and I suggest you do, add them here.
Sprinkle topping over fruit.

Bake for about 40 minutes, or until lightly browned.

Zelda's Plum Cake

Our dear friend Zelda Israel used to make this for Jewish holidays and other occasions. Though Zelda passed away years ago, I hope she would be pleased with my changes. The cake uses Italian prune plums which are only available in New Jersey in the early autumn. I like to make an extra plum cake while the plums are in season and freeze it for later in the year when we need a burst of brightening in the winter months.

1/3 cup canola oil
½ cup maple syrup
1 egg
2 tsp vanilla
2 tsp baking powder
1 tsp xanthan gum
4 Tbsp sweet rice flour
1 cup gluten-free flour mix
12 ripe small Italian prune plums, washed and dried

Topping
1 Tbsp maple sugar
1 Tbsp date sugar
1 tsp ground nutmeg
2 tsp cinnamon

Preheat oven to 400°. Oil a 6"x12" baking dish with canola oil.
Cut prune plums in half the long way and remove the pit.
Don't worry if they don't cut perfectly, it will look and taste great anyway.
In a small bowl, stir together the maple sugar, date sugar, nutmeg, and cinnamon, and set aside.
In a mixing bowl stir together canola oil and maple syrup.
Add egg and vanilla and stir well.
In a small bowl, combine the baking powder, xanthan gum, sweet rice flour, and gluten-free flour mix.
Add the dry ingredients to the wet ingredients and mix until it forms a dough.

Spread the dough in the prepared pan.
Press the plums into the dough cut-side down, leaving the purple backs of the plums showing.
Sprinkle the cake with all of the cinnamon-sugar mixture.
Bake the cake for 30-40 minutes or until a toothpick inserted into the center comes out clean.
The topping may be a bit bubbly.
Let cool to warm before serving.
Refrigerate any unused portions and re-warm before serving.

Vegan Lemon Bars

Developing this recipe required experimenting with several vegan recipes and some gluten-free ones as well. The result is a bar that has a more gel-like lemon topping, not gooey the way the sugary ones with lots of eggs would be. The topping has a darker yellow color than the kind made with white sugar but if you close your eyes they really do taste close to the "real" thing.

Crust
1 cup gluten-free flour mix
1 tsp xanthan gum
$\frac{1}{4}$ tsp sea salt
$\frac{1}{4}$ cup maple sugar
4 Tbsp Earth Balance or 3 Tbsp Earth Balance plus 1 Tbsp ghee

Lemon Topping
$\frac{3}{4}$ cup organic apple juice
$1\frac{1}{2}$ Tbsp agar agar flakes
1/3 cup fresh squeezed lemon juice
$1\frac{1}{2}$ Tbsp kuzu or arrowroot powder
6 Tbsp brown rice syrup
$\frac{1}{4}$ cup maple syrup
1/8 tsp ground turmeric
$1\frac{1}{2}$ tsp lemon zest
2 Tbsp plain soy milk

Desserts

To make the crust:
Combine all crust ingredients in the food processor and pulse until large crumbs are formed. Press this mixture into an 8x8 inch glass baking dish.
Bake at 350° for about 15 minutes. Remove from oven and set aside.

To make the filling:
Sprinkle the agar flakes on the apple juice in a small saucepan and let them soak for about 15 minutes while you prepare the other ingredients.
Squeeze the lemon juice and add the kuzu or arrowroot powder; stir to dissolve.
Zest the lemon rind and measure out $1\frac{1}{2}$ tsp and set aside.
Measure the brown rice syrup and maple syrup into a glass measuring pitcher.
Bring the agar and juice to a boil, turn down the heat to medium, and cook until the agar has completely dissolved, stirring with a wire whisk continuously. This can take about 10 minutes.
Keep the heat on medium and add the brown rice syrup and maple syrup and stir with the wire whisk to combine. Add the turmeric and stir.
Add the lemon juice mixed with kuzu or arrowroot. Stir to combine.
Add the lemon zest and soy milk and continue whisking.
Cook while whisking over medium heat about 7 minutes until the lemon topping thickens. It will still be pourable.

Pour the lemon topping over the crust and let it cool until barely warm then cover and refrigerate for a few hours before cutting into squares.
If you want to dress them up you can sprinkle some organic powdered sugar but they are delicious without the extra sugar.

Internet Sources

www.arrowheadmills.com
Gluten-free flours and baking mixes.

www.authenticfoods.com
This company makes the best <u>superfine</u> gluten-free flours and
flour mixes.
Order online and pay a well-worth-it shipping cost for finely
ground rice, corn, and sorghum flours. No more gritty baked
goods.

www.adriennesgourmetfoods.com
Papadini lentil pasta (high in protein) made from lentil flour,
baking soda, and salt.

www.babycakesnyc.com
Organic alternatives free from the common allergens: wheat,
gluten, dairy, casein and eggs. No white sugar or toxic chemical
sweeteners. Most products sweetened with agave nectar—a
natural syrup from a cactus. The bakery is located in the lower
east side, New York, and well worth the trip.

www.bobsredmill.com
Gluten-free flours, baking mixes, and cereals.

www.breakingtheviciouscycle.info
Specific carbohydrate diet information including complete list
of what to include and what to avoid. No starches or sugars
except honey. Certain cheeses and homemade yogurt are
allowed.

www.creamhillestates.com
Canadian certified gluten-free oats.

www.csaceliacs.org
Web site of the Celiac Sprue Association of the U.S. General information and printable information for restaurants, schools, etc.

www.eatingwell.com
Eating Well magazine web site with many easy and healthy recipes

www.ener-g.com
Gluten-free, dairy-free, egg-free, nut-free products.

www.enjoylifefoods.com
Dedicated gluten-free and peanut-free facility. Products are also free of the following allergens: dairy, casein, soy, corn, eggs, fish, shellfish. Products available online or in some stores including Whole Foods and some local natural food stores or groceries.

www.foodallergy.org
Food Allergy & Anaphylaxis Network. Great site for parents of children with food allergies.

www.gfcf.com
Gluten-free casein- free diet for autism spectrum. Recipes and ideas, chats and hints from parents. Gluten-free casein-free snack pack available to order.

www.giftsofnature.net
Certified gluten-free oats.

www.glutenfree.com
The Gluten-Free Pantry
Products listed by category (casein-free, egg-free, soy-free, etc)

www.glutenfree-supermarket.com
Authentic Foods brand products available as well as many others.

www.glutino.com
gluten-free/casein-free breads, crackers and cereal bars that you can purchase on line. Canadian company.

www.great-eastern-sun.com
Organic miso and sea vegetables.

www.healthycrowd.com
Nana's cookies. Some are gluten-free. No refined sugars, no dairy, no hydrogenated oils, no eggs.

www.kinnikinnick.com
gluten-free, casein-free baked goods.

www.larabar.com
Makers of foods bars that are gluten-free, dairy-free, refined-sugar-free. Delicious, convenient bars made from dates, nuts, natural flavors.

www.livingwithout.com
Gluten-free, dairy-free, chemical-free, allergy-free, yeast-free living. Recipes and lots of helpful information and tools. Magazine is quarterly.

www.minimus.biz
Search on "kari-out" for gluten-free soy sauce in individual packets. $0.11 per packet.

www.namastefoods.com
Makes foods that contain no wheat, gluten, corn, soy, potato, dairy, casein or nuts. Delicious brownie and cake mixes and my favorite gluten-free dairy-free mac n' cheese!

Internet Sources

www.newgrist.com
Lakefront Brewery gluten-free rice and sorghum beer available from Clubs of America by calling 1800-800-9122 (9-5 CDT, M-F). $35 including shipping for 12 bottles.

www.pamelasproducts.com
Mixes and cookies to order on line. Also available in grocery stores and Whole Foods.

www.perkysnaturalfoods.com
Gluten- and nut-free cereals.

www.rawganique.com
Raw foods including hemp food products.

www.redbridgebeer.com
Annheuser-Busch gluten-free beer made from rice and sorghum. Fairly wide distribution. Web site has tool for you to input your zip code to find a distributor near you.

www.scdrecipe.com
Specific carbohydrate diet recipes that only use honey as sweetener, no starches of any kind (no rice, potatoes, corn, grains, etc)

www.worldpantry.com
Living Harvest hemp seed products.

Acknowledgements

My parents raised me to believe that I could do anything that I set my mind to do. And I still believe it! Nevertheless, Melissa's Marvelous Meatless Meals would not be possible without the help and input of many people. To my friends and family who have helped, offered help, and provided so much support and inspiration, you are on these pages, and in my heart.

My parents, Ricki and Fred Bernstein, not only gave their unconditional love and encouragement, but thanks also go to my mom for her many hours of editing expertise, and to dad for his patience and photographic artistry.

Heartfelt thanks to Dr. Stuart Freedenfeld for writing the Foreword. You are a beacon in the medical world. I sincerely hope that more people will listen to us both.

Thanks to Reba Necky who helped me so much at the beginning of my family's gluten-free journey. Thank you to my recipe testers, the Sutch family, Susan Speak, and Ellen Pytlar, and to my Super testers Virginia Murphy and Sharyl Hoepfinger. Your input and suggestions were invaluable and your encouragement boosted my belief in this project. Thank you to Judy Downer for help with research into publishing firms. Sometimes you just have to get it done yourself.

Deb Gichan, you are an artist in every way. Thank you for loaning your kitchen for our photos and for sprinkling some of your magic talent over my project. Watching you work is like watching ballet. Thanks to Susan Speak for transitioning to food photos from turtle and wildlife photography. You make my food look good enough to eat. Lauren Zumpetta, from Action Fast Print, has the patience of a saint, a smile in her voice, and makes every customer feel like her only one.

To my children, Sarah and Josh, thank you for keeping open minds about all the weird food in our house, and encouraging me with "well, if mom made it, it must be tasty!" It's not easy to be different, but you both wear it extremely well.

And to Chris, my soul mate and the love of my life, thank you for your title which you wrote 25 years ago, for forcing me to go through with this project and guiding my first steps, for your lovely sketches, and for devoting so many hours to fighting with the software and putting it all together (how do you *know* these things?). It is a pleasure to cook for you and I look forward to many more years across the kitchen table.